About This Book

Why is this topic important?

Trainers increasingly are looking for interactive ways to engage trainees within a training session. Game shows are not only an effective way to review information, but they have been proven to help increase content retention, increase trainer engagement and interactivity, and get both trainers and trainees excited about training sessions. Game shows should be a tool in every trainer's tool box.

What can you achieve with this book?

When you are finished reading this book, you will:

• Be able to select, modify, and create your own training game show for maximum training impact.
• Have ideas for adding multimedia into your game show and using your game show in unique and creative ways.
• Know how to be the ultimate game show host, balanced with being the ultimate game show trainer.

How is this book organized?

This book is organized into four parts and is meant to be flipped through as you design your own game show and as you need to use each part:

Game Shows and Learning, where you'll find frequently asked questions, look at differences between training game shows and TV game shows, understand the brain-based theory behind game shows, and know the common game show misconceptions.
Designing a Game Show for Learning, where you'll find the nuts and bolts of creating your own game show, including game show descriptions, game show selections and customizations, and setting the game show rules.

Writing Effective Questions, where you'll explore different types of questions, tips for writing questions, and using multimedia in questions.

Conducting a Game Show, where you'll find tips for hosting while training, maximizing learning in your game show, setting up for the game show, game show software and hardware options, and guides to rate your game show and give yourself feedback.

In addition, the **Resources** section contains helpful books and sources for software, hardware, and premade game show materials.

About Pfeiffer

Pfeiffer serves the professional development and hands-on resource needs of training and human resource practitioners and gives them products to do their jobs better. We deliver proven ideas and solutions from experts in HR development and HR management, and we offer effective and customizable tools to improve workplace performance. From novice to seasoned professional, Pfeiffer is the source you can trust to make yourself and your organization more successful.

Essential Knowledge Pfeiffer produces insightful, practical, and comprehensive materials on topics that matter the most to training and HR professionals. Our Essential Knowledge resources translate the expertise of seasoned professionals into practical, how-to guidance on critical workplace issues and problems. These resources are supported by case studies, worksheets, and job aids and are frequently supplemented with CD-ROMs, websites, and other means of making the content easier to read, understand, and use.

Essential Tools Pfeiffer's Essential Tools resources save time and expense by offering proven, ready-to-use materials—including exercises, activities, games, instruments, and assessments—for use during a training or team-learning event. These resources are frequently offered in loose-leaf or CD-ROM format to facilitate copying and customization of the material.

Pfeiffer also recognizes the remarkable power of new technologies in expanding the reach and effectiveness of training. While e-hype has often created whizbang solutions in search of a problem, we are dedicated to bringing convenience and enhancements to proven training solutions. All our e-tools comply with rigorous functionality standards. The most appropriate technology wrapped around essential content yields the perfect solution for today's on-the-go trainers and human resource professionals.

Pfeiffer
www.pfeiffer.com   Essential resources for training and HR professionals

I'll Take Learning for 500

I'll Take Learning for 500

Using Game Shows to Engage, Motivate, and Train

Dan Yaman and Missy Covington

Foreword by Sivasailam "Thiagi" Thiagarajan

Pfeiffer

A Wiley Imprint
www.pfeiffer.com

Copyright page continued on page 239.

Library of Congress Cataloging-in-Publication Data

Yaman, Dan
 I'll take learning for 500 : using game shows to engage, motivate, and train / Dan Yaman and Missy Covington.
   p. cm.
 Includes bibliographical references and index.
 ISBN-13: 978-0-7879-8306-2 (pbk.)
 ISBN-10: 0-7879-8306-3 (pbk.)
 1. Employees—Training of. 2. Game shows. 3. Training. I. Covington, Missy, II. Title.
 HF5549.5.T7Y36 2006
 658.3'124—dc22
                        2006006226

Acquiring Editor: Lisa Shannon   Manufacturing Supervisor: Becky Carreño
Director of Development: Kathleen Dolan Davies   Editorial Assistant: Jesse C. Wiley
Production Editor: Nina Kreiden   Illustrations: Dan Kelly
Editor: Bev Miller

Printed in the United States of America
Paperback Printing   10 9 8 7 6 5 4 3 2 1

Contents

Part Two: Designing a Game Show for Learning

CD Content

Foreword

By Sivasailam "Thiagi" Thiagarajan

I will not waste your time repeating the why, what, and how of game shows that my friends Dan and Missy have so eloquently explained in the following pages. Instead, let me make three simple points based on more than thirty years of designing and conducting game shows around the world:

1. Validated laws of learning support the use of game shows.
2. Game shows blend polar factors.
3. Game shows have limitations that can be creatively managed.

Law and Order

I have spent several years deriving suitable training prescriptions from experimental laws of learning. Let me give you a sample of two such laws that support the use of game shows as a training tool:

- The law of emotional learning states that *events that elicit emotions result in long-lasting learning.* This law suggests that people learn when they are happy or sad or angry. But they do not learn when they are in a state of boredom or apathy. Playful elements and healthy competition during game shows add an emotional element, without becoming so intense as to interfere with learning.

- The law of practice and feedback states that *learners cannot master concepts and skills without repeated practice and relevant feedback*. This law emphasizes that passive understanding of content does not guarantee recall and application. With the use of a large number of questions and immediate feedback with reinforcement, game shows ensure meaningful practice and relevant feedback.

Blending Is Better Than Balancing

Beginning trainers (and sometimes experienced trainers too) ask useless *either-or* questions, such as "Which is better: competition or cooperation?" The obvious answer is that both factors contribute to learning. To leverage this fact, some trainers attempt to strike a happy medium by balancing the extremes. This usually results in a bland and boring combination. Fortunately, however, game shows permit a blending of opposing factors, thus enabling us to have the *chapatti* and eat it too.

Let's return to cooperation and competition. Here's how game shows leverage both these motivators: Rivalry among teams tap into the competitive mode. This also results in an intense level of cooperation among the members of each team.

Let's explore chance and skill. If winning a game depends on pure chance, there is no need for players to master new concepts and skills. On the other hand, if success in the game depends purely on recall and skill, players who have fallen behind lose hope and give up learning. An effective game show blends skill (example: recall of information) with chance elements (example: doubling of scores during the second round) to keep the players continuously engaged.

Let's move on to individuals and teams. Teams encourage participants to learn with (and learn from) each other. But at the same time, they reduce the need for individual responsibility for learning. An effective game show blends these modes by alternating team preparation with individual contest (between randomly selected team members).

Passive and active participation presents another interesting challenge. The brain shuts down after lengthy periods of passive listening and burns out after hectic activity. An effective game show appropriately alternates between passive content presentation and active competitive play to blend these two opposing modes.

The key to effective design and facilitation of game shows is to skillfully blend these and several other opposing polarities.

Beyond Game Shows

I am fond of telling trainers that they are limited to only three occasions in a training session for the use of game shows: before, during, and after. I hasten to explain that we can use game shows before training to excite participants and to discover what they already know. After training, we can use game shows to review the content and test participants. During training, we can use games to integrate what the participants are learning with what they have already learned.

An important instructional principle lies behind this flippant remark (and the simple-minded explanation): Game shows perform a necessary function in the teaching-learning process, but they are not sufficient in themselves. Game shows encourage participants to recall relevant content while answering questions. However, they do not provide the content in the first place. The total training session must include some method for presenting content: a lecture, a videotape, a handout, a reading assignment, or conversations among participants. Game shows can be interspersed before, during, and after these content presentation activities to provide practice and feedback.

Even in the area of providing practice and feedback, game shows have a critical limitation: They typically focus on factual and conceptual learning by using closed questions for which there are single correct answers. Real life, however, is full of wicked problems featuring open-ended questions that permit a wide range of acceptable answers. What we require of participants is creative application of newly learned principles and procedures. Traditional game shows do not encourage such thinking outside the box. However, with some ingenuity, we can come up with game shows that reward creative responses (as judged by experts, audience members, or peers). We can also supplement game shows with other interactive instructional strategies, such as action learning, the case method, coaching, debriefing, dialogues, discussions, group projects, field work, improv activities, interactive story-telling, journaling, reflection, role plays, and simulations.

Game shows are efficient and enjoyable in what they do. They must be integrated with other training activities to ensure effective learning that produces real-world results.

Introduction: Why We Wrote This Book

We want to improve your experience as a trainer, and we believe that all training can be improved with game shows. This is an equal opportunity book: the game shows that we describe should be a component of every type, shape, size, color, and creed of training.

Game shows enrich both the trainer and the trainees' experience in a training class. Remember the saying, "If mamma ain't happy, ain't nobody happy"? This holds true in training. If the trainees are bored, then you won't be happy. If you're not happy, there's no way the trainees are going to be excited about their training. It's really a vicious cycle.

Our purpose in writing this book is to stop that cycle. We don't have a twelve-step program, but we do have this comprehensive guide to using game shows in the training classroom. This book will show you how to leverage the excitement and entertainment inherent in game shows. Using game shows will increase participant involvement as well as information retention and comprehension. Game shows are not a spectator sport or a diversion; they are a powerful learning tool. This book will help you to select, create, modify, and employ game shows in powerful, effective ways. Your training may never be the same again.

A Tale of Two Classrooms

Classroom A

I'm sure we've all seen Classroom A somewhere in our life experience. Perhaps this is even what some people think of when they hear the words "training course."

Imagine there is one trainer facing fifteen trainees. The trainer is lecturing on very important material that the trainees need to know to do their jobs. Four of the trainees are doodling in their manuals, two are writing notes to each other in the margins, one of them is just starting to snooze lightly, six of the trainees look catatonic, one other trainee is checking her calendar on an electronic organizer, and one trainee is maybe, just maybe, at full attention. The lecture is very traditional, and even the trainer is starting to look bored. The material is interspersed with, "I'm sorry, but we have to go through this—it's policy," and "We have to get up to speed so we can pass compliance; don't worry, we're almost done." The trainees walk out of the room looking like extras in a 1950s B-movie Zombie thriller—only there's nothing thrilling about them. The concern is not whether they remember the material, but that they were present for the training session.

Frankly, most people get tired just *reading* about Classroom A.

Classroom B

Perhaps we've seen Classroom B as well, experienced bits and pieces of it in our training, and are energized just thinking about it.

Imagine there is one trainer facing fifteen trainees. The trainer is playing a game show based around important material that the trainees need to know to do their jobs. The trainees are split into three teams of five, and as the trainer reads off the first question with a style that Alex Trebek himself would envy, the three teams jump to answer first. Team 2 was first: they discuss the material briefly and answer the question. Teams 1 and 3 express some chagrin at not being able to answer the question, but they listen attentively. Team 2 answers the question wrong, and teams 1 and 3 come alive in a frenzy of motion. Team 3 buzzes in and answers the question correctly.

All of a sudden the room erupts into cheering. The atmosphere is electric, and the trainer awards points to team 3. After the question, the teams discuss why that was the correct answer with the trainer. Then it's on to question 2. In no time, the class is over and the trainees leave the room with high fives and congratulations. After they get out of the room, one of the trainees says to another, "So what did you think about that final question?" The trainer smiles, feeling as though they had just climbed to the top of Mount

Everest—the trainees are talking about the material even *after* the training session. The trainees remember the material and are excited to go back to work and apply the knowledge that they have just gained.

Here's the kicker: Classroom B is a completely real scenario. We've met dozens of trainers who have Classroom A experiences and have literally transformed the attitude, mind-set, and learning capacity of their trainees by adding game shows to their training. The trainees who were reluctant to go to a training session became excited about playing a learning game show.

Using games in the training or school classroom is not a new concept. Teachers have long been incorporating games to increase learning and add energy to material. Remember spelling bees, flash cards, maybe even skits and presentations? These are all games that inspired students to pay attention, remember, and apply material. Game *shows*, however, are unique in their ability to help trainers and trainees get the most out of their training. In the next chapter, we'll tell you how.

First Things First . . .

To get the most out of this book, there are several ways to use it.

Look back at the Contents and pick the chapter that you need; then skip around after that. This book is a tool, and reading straight through it is not necessary. Each chapter is self-contained and can be read alone.

Nevertheless, this book can be even more useful by reading straight through it. You might find answers to questions you didn't even know you had. If you've never used game shows in your training or classroom experience, you'll find useful tips along the way. If you're a game show expert, you may discover different ways of applying and improving your game shows.

Throughout this book you'll find our tips and tricks and are bound to stumble on things that require some further explanation. We have identified these items as follows:

Case Studies—Real experiences and solutions from real trainers who use game shows regularly in their training.

 More Information—For when you want to know just a little bit more. This is where you might find brain-based learning theory, explanations, or extra information on a topic.

 Tips—These boxes offer a shortcut to finding out what works for you when using game shows in training.

Part I

Game Shows and Learning

The chapters in Part One walk you through some of the science and philosophy behind the effectiveness of game shows. We want you to understand why game shows are such a useful tool and give you a taste of their versatility. You may have doubts and apprehensions about using game shows in your training, and we'll explore those concerns as well. If someone should ask you why you're "playing games" in your training, you can reply that it's because games are one of the most highly effective ways to engage adult learners.

Chapter 1

Classroom vs. Hollywood

How Training Game Shows Differ from TV Game Shows

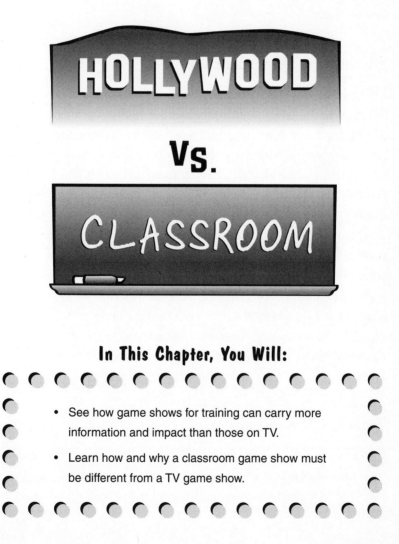

In This Chapter, You Will:

- See how game shows for training can carry more information and impact than those on TV.
- Learn how and why a classroom game show must be different from a TV game show.

The game shows that we watch on TV are for entertainment—that's why we enjoy them so much. We can share in the glory and the tragedy of the contestants and try to answer questions along with them. However, for *learning* game shows to be effective, they need to be more than just entertaining. The trainer needs to take liberties with the rules and the format. We must emphasize that training game shows have fundamental differences from their television cousins and that these differences are necessary for them to be effective.

Education vs. Entertainment

While it's fun to watch a game show on TV and you may remember a few of the trivia questions and answers after the show, generally we don't learn anything from watching a television game show. Any knowledge a contestant displays on a game show is viewed as extraordinary or incidental; what is missing is training. On TV there is no time to review an incorrect question, no time to elaborate on material related to an answer, no major topic that content is centered around (instead you have a compilation of random trivia), and no real link to tie the whole fantastic spectacle into real-world applications. So what if another contestant knows that a crampon is a spiked climbing boot. Are you going to remember and apply that after you get home? Not unless you're taking up mountain climbing. A classroom game show allows you to review, elaborate, correct, and apply your content, as well as place it in a real-world scenario.

Teams vs. Contestants

Instead of individual contestants playing against each other, training game shows use teams. The idea is to get as many people involved in training as possible. By grouping players together on a team you:

- Increase collaboration and participation.

- Create a bond between trainees and increase the feeling of camaraderie.

- Limit the embarrassment a person may feel answering a question alone because the entire team is responsible for an answer.

- Leave no room for someone to "check out" and hide in the back. Every team member's contributions are a crucial part of the team effort, and each is held accountable by teammates.

- Give trainees the opportunity to learn from, and to teach, their own peers.

You may also take liberties with the number of teams playing the game. Just because TV's *Jeopardy!* has three contestants doesn't mean you have to have three teams; you can have four or five if it suits the size of your training class. While TV's *Who Wants to Be a Millionaire?* has just one contestant at a time, you will need to have more than one team for your *Millionaire* game.

Classroom game shows also give you the opportunity to use an audience. In a TV game show, not only is the audience not involved, but they are actively encouraged not to participate, although they are told when to clap politely and when to laugh. In your training game, you can use the audience to increase the energy of a game show by cheering and being part of the teams, giving answers, demonstrating procedures, and contributing to the learning process.

Trainer vs. Quizmaster

Although hosting and keeping the game running smoothly is an important part of a game show, never underestimate the crucial importance of training. We will note the significance of providing additional background and content before, during, and after a question to increase the amount that trainees learn and absorb. *Your role is not just to facilitate the game show but also to support the contestants and ensure that learning is taking place.* We daresay that your job is a bit more difficult—and has a greater impact—than any commercial game show host who just reads questions and relates whether the answers are correct or incorrect.

Encouragement vs. Embarrassment

While most game shows seek to cheer the winners and soothe the losers, some recent game shows, such as *The Weakest Link*, have been downright nasty to the losers. People learn best in a supportive and nurturing environment. The host-trainer should never insult or tease a trainee in an unpleasant manner. Although there is competition in a learning game show, the focus should be on what was learned, not who won the game. We want students to leave with knowledge above all, not necessarily victory.

Function vs. Flair

If you want to incorporate stage lighting, elaborate costuming, and large prizes into your training session, we're not going to stop you, but we advise you against it in general. A lot of extraneous elements often detract from the main objective: your trainees' learning. In the case of training games, the most memorable items should be the questions and answers, not the music and lights (unless, of course, your training includes lighting or music recognition). Your game show can be spiced up, but don't make it a grand production unless that is specifically its purpose. We say this because a training game show doesn't need all the extras to be effective. A simple setting can provide more opportunities to learn than one would expect.

Your Rules vs. TV Rules

The great thing about a game show is that it is ultimately flexible. Game shows are just formats to which you add your own content, teams, and rules. There's nothing wrong with revising some (or all) of the rules in a game show providing you specify the rule changes in advance. In fact, TV rules don't always work well in a training scenario or may not be realistic with the size or type of your group. For instance, although TV's *Jeopardy!* requires a contestant to ring in to answer, you may find it more beneficial to alternate which team gets to select a question and give an answer. If a team is far behind halfway through the game, you may have a rule that allows teams to earn extra points by demonstrating a skill. The key is announcing any such rule at the beginning of the game.

Your Way vs. Their Way

Ultimately the game show is yours. Don't be afraid to change the way the game is played. It is only the tool; you decide the best way to use a tool for it to be effective. For example, in *Wheel of Fortune*, you can require contestants to correctly answer a question prior to guessing a letter. *Who Wants to Be a Millionaire?* uses only multiple-choice questions, but that doesn't mean that you can't make them open-ended or ask the contestants to perform a physical skill or action. Change the game any way you choose, but keep it relatively simple, and explain the rules to your trainees before they start playing the game.

———

As you can see, TV game shows, while an inherently entertaining game show base, need modification before they are brought into a training classroom. Many of these modifications are small, but can make a large difference in how your trainees absorb and retain the game show information (you'll see more about customizing a game show in Chapters Six through Eight). However, the game show base can work wonders in your training session, as you'll see in the next chapter.

Chapter 2

Why Use a Game Show?

In This Chapter, You Will:

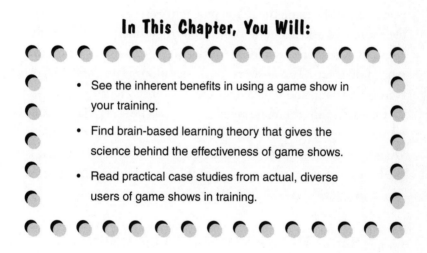

- See the inherent benefits in using a game show in your training.

- Find brain-based learning theory that gives the science behind the effectiveness of game shows.

- Read practical case studies from actual, diverse users of game shows in training.

To understand the basic reason that game shows are effective training tools, read the following three sentences:

- How many feet are in 10 yards?

- Name the first person to walk on the moon.

- What is the first word in the body of the Gettysburg Address?

As you were reading the questions, were you answering them in your head at the same time? You probably were. A majority of people cannot be asked a question without their brains automatically going into gear and searching for the answer or reflecting on the type of question. The answers to the questions above are: 30 feet, Neil Armstrong, and four. Were your answers correct?

Questions are the building blocks of a game show. They allow trainees to test themselves, challenge their peers, and compete for knowledge in a fun way. While the question-and-answer format is the basic attraction to game shows, there are many other benefits of playing game shows in the training classroom.

Game Shows Review Without Calling It a Review

Game shows don't scream rehash or boredom. When you say "review," the first thought that comes to some people's minds is "boring." If information has just been presented in a training session, the prospect of having to review it is downright tedious. It's true that we humans need things said multiple times in order to firmly implant them in our memory. However, reviewing information need not mean rereading a manual out loud or lecturing a second time on material. By using a game show to review, you incorporate fun into learning. Reviewing is an opportunity for trainees to show what they know. Reviewing should normally take up a large chunk of time, and that time must be used effectively.

Case Study: Game Show Reviews

Candace, the training director for a large building company, had to make sure that a high number of trainees passed their licensing exams. After all, if the trainees didn't pass, they would lose their jobs. After a day and a half of class, the participants were understandably overwhelmed with the new responsibility that they had. They had to comply with all the new rules, policies, and procedures and absorb a great deal of information, plus worry about passing the exam at the end of the training. These conditions were not conducive to producing the best test results. Candace and her fellow trainers were dedicated to the success of the trainees and sought ways to conduct review sessions before the exams so that trainees could be as relaxed and confident about the material as possible. They decided to use game shows.

Candace describes the results, "'Playing' the game show really makes a difference. I have had many students tell me after the exam that they would never have passed without playing the review game. They could even remember who answered what question and whether they answered it correctly in the game show."

We've had trainees report to us remembering exact questions and answers years after playing a game show. That's a review that trainers can take to the bank.

Games Shows Are Great for Test Preparation

Game shows allow you to prepare for an exam in a low-pressure way or sneak in an exam or evaluation without trainees ever knowing that they are being tested. Reviewing with game shows using questions similar to those that will be on the exam is beneficial to trainees' learning. Adequate preparation also reduces test anxiety. Using a game show to review can both alleviate pressure with its fun method of review and help trainees feel more prepared for their exams. The results that Candace reported in the case study were extraordinary: 63 percent more people passed using game shows to prepare for their exams than those who had only oral reviews.

Game Shows Are a Strong Preview Mechanism

A learning game show is an effective way to preview material that you are about to cover. If your trainees already have had some experience with the topic, either on the job or in the real world, then accessing and using those experiences by playing a game show will prepare them for the training session. To prime the trainees, you don't necessarily need to use specific content; all you have to do is create a spark of thought around a topic. This elevates trainees into the state where they are ready and willing to learn. For example, if you were going to train in specific safety procedures, a game can get them thinking about the many different ways that employees can hurt themselves, what unsafe work conditions mean for a business, or how automated safety procedures could save them time with their hazard reporting.

Game shows can also create curiosity among the trainees. They become excited and inquisitive about the material you're going to present. You could ask, for example, "What are the five best ways to handle a customer complaint?" Chances are your participants won't be able to name all five ways or they'll give some incorrect answers. Then they will wonder what the correct answers are and why those answers are correct. Game shows are a springboard for diving into a topic and kick-starting discussion in a training session.

 Preview Isn't Just for the Beginning

Preview at:

- *Midday* to introduce a new unit or topic. Sometimes trainers find that it helps to break up training topics during a session. For example, if you are training on improving customer service, you might have modules like new policies, dealing with customer objections, going above and beyond, and effects of good customer service. If all of these modules are taught right after another with no break, they may blend together in the mind of the trainee. Putting a game show in between each module can serve as a preview to a new topic, priming and preparing the trainees to head in a new direction.

- *The end of the day* to prepare and prime for the next training session. If you have multiday training sessions, game shows can be a useful preview for the next day's material. We've seen trainees stumble out of the classroom, numbed by information and thinking, *Do I have to go through another day of this!?* Because game shows can generate curiosity and excitement about a topic, trainees have something to look forward to in the next training session and will feel more knowledgeable about the upcoming topic.

Game Shows Can Make Participants Aware of Their Own Strengths and Weaknesses

Inevitably there will be someone who is new, inexperienced, or less knowledgeable who will come into a training course with an *I feel so stupid, I don't know anything* attitude that unfortunately sets up a mental learning block. A game show is a nonthreatening way to introduce information. Even if the trainee has to guess an answer, he or she will start to see that learning the information isn't so difficult. The trainee may also know some of the answers through experience or intuition; in this case, he or she will feel empowered and ready to go on with the training.

If your trainees think they "know it all," playing a game show can create awareness of what they would personally like to find out about a topic, or surprise them with what they don't know yet (or shut them up quickly if they're being particularly obnoxious about their perceived knowledge).

Game Shows Energize the Class and Generate Positive Emotions

Game shows mix people up, force them to get out of their seats, and get them to participate. The interaction of the question-and-answer format doesn't allow trainees to check out of the learning equation. Because they are involved, they become responsible for their own learning and for the training. It cannot be a one-sided training session with minimal participation; it is a lively session where everyone is involved.

Our emotions dictate a gigantic proportion of our lives, from how we react to others, to what decisions we make, to what kinds of products we buy. It is no surprise that emotions also have an impact on how we learn. Someone who is in a bad mood during training will remember the overall training experience as negative or chalk it up to having a bad day and dismiss it altogether (Jensen, 1995).

Eric Jensen (1995, p. 38) says in his book, *The Learning Brain,* "When we are feeling positive we are able to sort out our experiences better and recall with more clarity." In lay terms, this means that the more positive we feel, the better experience we think we have and the more accurately we recall and remember information. This means that it is very important to bring positive experiences into a training session.

Game shows engage learners in a way that is fun—but they're not fun for fun's sake. After all, the content of the training is serious. Nevertheless, the act of playing a game show helps trainees to relax and absorb the information. They then see your content through the rose-colored glasses of a positive experience. In turn they remember more of the content and feel good about their training class.

 Game Shows Are (Literally) a Moving Experience

Extensive research in brain-based learning has found that simply standing up for a few moments can increase blood flow to the brain and allow us to learn more effectively. Even something as simple as having good posture can allow better flow of oxygen and can contribute to being more alert and focused on the material at hand. Trainees who are slumped over and sitting for extended periods of time can get listless and bored, even if the material is gripping (Jensen, 1995).

Game shows give people an excuse to move around in the training space. That doesn't mean that trainees are out of control; rather, they are participating in a physical way. They can move to another side of the room to form teams, may have to raise their hands or make a noise to "ring in" for a question, can act out or explain their answers in the game, draw their answers on a whiteboard, or just cheer for their successes. There is a wealth of possibilities in a game show for incorporating physical movement that will keep trainees alert.

Game Show Competition Motivates the Trainee

While some trainers may shy away from competition in favor of collaboration, game shows can effectively blend both competition and collaboration. People in general are eager to prove how much they know. They are particularly willing to demonstrate that their spectrum of knowledge is greater than another person's. Competition is in our biological makeup. (The fastest runner gets the prey, after all.) Introducing an element of competition inspires people to participate and collaborate; they want to jump right into the game and show what they know.

If participants know that a game show is going to be played at the end of a training session, the element of competition will motivate them to pay attention to the material. No one wants to look as if they aren't pulling their weight or haven't been paying attention. Having a game show in training makes them responsible for learning the content. Playing a game show may also inspire your trainees to go above and beyond to learn more about the content at hand.

Case Study: Motivating the Student

Linda, an instructional designer at a community college, started using game shows in her training sessions with students and faculty. Her content ranges from mathematical statistics and science to ecology and anatomy. She explains her experience using game shows: "We have some 'jocks' and some other students here who had barely opened a book. Now that we have started playing game shows that use elements of competition, they're cracking the books like I've never seen before." Students were studying material outside the classroom in order to do well playing the game shows.

Game Shows Provide Feedback for the Trainer and Trainee

For the trainer, using a game show can gauge what students have absorbed in the training session and what they're not getting. For example, if trainees return blank stares in response to a game show question; consistently get the same question, subjects, or topics wrong; or can't explain their answer in an open-ended question, those responses show the trainer that the content in question should be emphasized in the training session. Trainers can then choose to do extra review or skip over the material that everyone seems to understand. They can figure out where the skill gaps are and what topics don't need any further explanation.

For the student, a game show gives immediate feedback about what they do and do not know, leaving them confident in their abilities, eager to know what they don't already and sure about what they need to study. They also know exactly what they are responsible for taking out of the training session and what the trainer is expecting of them. This leads to students' feeling more secure about the training and more supportive of the instructor.

Game Shows Promote Teamwork

Game shows give trainees an easy opportunity to interact with each other and encourage them to use their teammates as resources. They can be a bonding experience for members of a division or group and can help new people mesh with an established or existing group of trainees. Using game shows within an established work environment encourages interoffice networking and can build stronger working relationships between and within departments.

Putting trainees into teams during a game show and encouraging them to collaborate on answers paves the way for increased learning. Teams that are allowed to discuss an answer within a game show have an advantage over trainees who listen to a lecture alone. The act of discussing their ideas with their peers, hashing through misunderstandings, and developing one coherent team answer has been proven to increase topic understanding and allow them to better integrate information into their real-world experiences (Jensen, 1995).

Game Shows Can Help Clarify Material

Game shows allow trainers to pause and expound on particular points or material at times of peak attention. For example, say you just asked the question, "What type of organic soil conditioner should you use when planting a new evergreen tree?" The answer is "peat moss." Your extra information could include something like: "Peat moss is essential to retain moisture, fertilize, and loosen hard soils." The contestant gave the "what" answer, but in order for it to stick most effectively, participants have to know the "why."

Game Shows Are Ideal for Addressing All Kinds of Issues

There are some training topics that are fairly standard but that no one really wants to talk about—even though they are included in mandatory training. Sexual harassment is not exactly a jump-around-

and-get-excited-about-it topic. Playing a game show will allow you to prepare trainees for the topic in a nonthreatening way that doesn't take away from its seriousness. If you get trainees thinking about sexual harassment through the focus of positive emotion (as they experience in a game show), they will be able to talk more candidly and honestly about any problems or issues around the subject. This can also work for topics like bad sales years and company problems. We're not talking about a *Jeopardy!* category like "Who's Getting Laid Off," but we are suggesting using the game shows as a segue to developing open communication and problem solving around such issues.

Game Shows Cover Multiple Learning Styles

Game shows appeal to multiple learning styles. Whatever their learning style classification, all people learn through their senses; what differs from person to person is which sense they favor. Game shows are a multisensory experience. Whereas one person may benefit from a lecture, or verbal style of instruction, the lesson may fall on deaf ears for someone who learns better by seeing pictures, shapes, and diagrams. Game shows accommodate all of the sensory learning styles.

 **Game Shows and the Senses**

Game shows have an inherent **visual** interest. Contestants read the questions, can watch their scores tally, and can view graphics, movies, pictures, or diagrams that are part of the game show. Trainees are also able to see the correct answer, cementing it in their mind.

Game shows are **auditory**. Contestants hear the question, read it to their teammates, communicate with their team, hear spoken answers, and listen to the sounds, songs, and any game show sound effects.

Game shows are hands-on, or **kinesthetic**. Contestants move around, raise their hands, demonstrate an answer, act out a scenario, and ring in.

Game shows can be **tasty** and **fragrant** too! If you are training chefs to recognize herbs, you can bring in samples and attach them to particular questions in the game show where they can taste or smell their way to a high score.

The point is that no matter how your trainees' brains work to absorb information, a game show has flexibility and variety to appeal to a room full of different learners without leaving anyone senseless.

Game Shows Bridge Generation Gaps

Game shows appeal to multiple generations. If I were to say the word *Jeopardy!* in the context of a game, pretty much everyone over age ten would know what I was referring to. Game shows have become part of American culture and have been integrated into many other cultures as well through the medium of television.

Case Study: Bridging the Generation Gap

Often the employees in a single business are at different levels of experience, knowledge, ages, and even generations. Trainers at a large pipeline corporation had to find a way to include all staff members—new, experienced, young, or old—in safety training. Introducing game shows as a training tool was met with some skepticism, but in the end it proved to unite the Gen X-ers and the baby boomers. "Using the game show creates a great learning environment," says Roger, one of the trainers. "It's very interesting to watch older and younger fellows mix so well; it's really a lot of fun. At first we always have a mixed reaction from people about 'playing games,' but as the day progresses, our biggest naysayers become our biggest cheerleaders."

The game show helped bridge the generation gap by uniting the different individuals toward a common goal on an equal playing field. We all have a little bit of kid in us, whether we're fifteen or eighty-five— and that kid is naturally drawn to play.

Game Shows Are a Change of Pace and Energizer for the Trainer

Let's not forget about the benefits to the trainer. We all know that happy trainers make happy and *educated* trainees. Chances are that you're going to be more motivated and positive if your trainees are excited about training than if they are just passing through and grumbling all the way. Game shows can help generate that excitement. Although game shows are a useful and fundamental tool, we can't forget to emphasize that they are *fun*. Game shows are enjoyable (and easy!) to host, and it's a break from putting together a lecture.

Case Study: Material Revisited

We interviewed John, a trainer for the Federal Bureau of Prisons who had been using game shows in his training program. He rotates about a hundred prison employees each week in multiple training sessions. The training is basically the same hygiene and health modules with each group, each day, every week, every month, and every year.

John explains: "It's hard as an instructor to get up there in front of people who you know are not interested in your information. Annual mandatory training is *much* better using game shows. Since some of these people have been working in the prison for twenty years and the material doesn't change, it gets very boring. With the game show, we get a big boost in training; people actually give excellent reviews versus the previous years' very neutral or negative reviews. Game shows are very interactive, and everyone loves them. Even our trainers love them, and now we use these game shows for *everything*! It takes a lot of the pressure off our instructors."

Although the information was the same, the training was the same, and the trainers were the same, it took a load off the trainers' minds to have a captive, excited audience. It became fun to present the information with game shows.

Game shows add variety to every training session—even with the same material. You never know which team is going to win, who will come up with new and innovative answers, and which personalities you will meet. We'll explore more tips on making your game show experience the best, most effective, and fun experience that it can be in Part Four on hosting a game show.

Game Shows Redefine the Perception of Training

Game shows are not just a forgettable spot in the fabric of a training session. They're an event. They allow people to be interactive, engaged, social, and competitive, and learn all at the same time. That type of multisensory engagement is something people remember. We've heard countless reports of trainers having trainees walk into their classroom and ask if they were going to play "that game show" again or brag about still remembering which question they won with last year. Training was already fun, but game shows add an interactive dynamic that is unmatched.

Trainers who have their trainees fill out evaluations at the end of a training session find that their evaluation scores improve significantly when they use game shows and that the trainees appreciate their efforts to make the training session fun and interactive. Game shows break the training mold and dispel the myth that to train means to lecture.

Game Shows Increase Retention

All of the benefits listed add up to one *very important* benefit: the bottom line, which is that game shows increase trainees' content retention.

Case Study: The ERC University Story

ERC Properties, Inc., a large real estate development firm, trains information that is not exactly intrinsically captivating but is vital to its employees' job performance. Training sessions are mandatory and include strict federal regulations, development housing regulations, sales and marketing, human resources, and ERC trivia. Employees' jobs literally depend on passing the regulation exams that follow their training.

"To my surprise, the more difficult the regulations, the better they seemed to fit into the games, and the easier they were to comprehend," said Candace, an ERC training director, "I believe it was because building the game made it necessary for me to break down the information into small pieces. These chunks of information were small enough for almost anyone to understand and retain." After using the game shows for a while, Candace and her fellow trainers started measuring the results of the classes where they used game shows versus those where they did not—but orally reviewed the same material. The results: an average of 88 percent of trainees passed the exams when using a game show to do review versus an average of 54 percent passing without using the game show.

Game shows have proven themselves to be effective tools in the training classroom. Even with the wealth of information and support behind game shows, there are still some common myths and misconceptions. We'll explore those, along with frequently asked questions, in the next chapter.

Chapter 3

Myths, Misconceptions, and Frequently Asked Questions

In This Chapter, You Will:

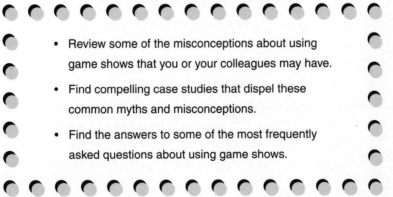

- Review some of the misconceptions about using game shows that you or your colleagues may have.

- Find compelling case studies that dispel these common myths and misconceptions.

- Find the answers to some of the most frequently asked questions about using game shows.

Some of the following objections to using game shows may sound fairly familiar to you. You or your colleagues may be having some of these reactions right now: "Sure, game shows sound great, but they'll never work for me because . . . [insert excuse here]." In this chapter we expose those objections for what they really are: misconceptions.

Myth 1: A Game Show Wouldn't Appeal to My Trainees . . . They're Too Shy, Too Professional, Too Blue Collar, Too Serious.

Truth: Games have the uncanny ability to engage even the shyest, most skeptical, or most professional of trainees. Everyone from a white-collar executive to a blue-collar factory line worker likes to have fun and compete. They will appreciate a training experience that is exciting and engaging.

Game shows have multiple elements that appeal to a wide spectrum of people, from the most competitive salesperson to the shyest "newbie." They include competition, socialization, fun, learning, and a chance to express themselves and their knowledge.

Case Study: A Game for All Kinds

One wouldn't expect a bunch of utility workers or miners to get excited about training or playing a game show. David, a safety supervisor for an electric company, learned otherwise after bringing game shows into his classroom. "In the end, everyone thinks that the game show is the neatest thing," says David. "The competition of the game show tends to show what they [the trainees] know." The game show capitalizes on the personality traits of his workers: "Because they know they're going to be tested on the material it makes them want to learn and remember more. There's a large amount of peer pressure involved as well. We had a guy the other day who no one thought knew anything, but when we started playing the game shows, we learned that he really knew a lot."

It's human nature to be competitive, and capitalizing on this trait is highly effective in a training session, no matter what the content is.

Whether trainees are young or old, inexperienced or seasoned, professional or laid back, executives or janitors, we have never run into a case where game shows haven't been used effectively and, in the end, received positively.

Myth 2: They Won't Work for My Subject . . . It's Too Technical or Too Sensitive to Have Fun.

Truth: Game shows can take a subject that is particularly touchy, tough, and tedious and transform it into a truly tantalizing training experience. Any subject can be made into a game show. Later in this book, you'll see how you can tailor your game shows specifically to teach your type of content.

Case Study: From Avoidance to Interaction

Quincy and George are instructional designers for major universities. Quincy uses game shows to train students and staff members in his college residence halls. The purpose of his training includes introducing new information *and* dispelling certain myths about serious topics such as sexual health, alcohol education, cancer awareness, diversity awareness, racism recognition, sexism recognition, homophobia awareness, and multicultural holidays. Quincy notes, "Some of these topics are particularly touchy. When we've had staff training sessions without using a game show, there tends to be this long, awkward, painful silence. Using game shows just sort of clears the air so that we can start talking about things." Some of the previous topics could be uncomfortable to present in conventional ways. Using game shows allows somber topics to be dealt with directly but in a way that is not awkward or embarrassing.

George covers topics like sexual awareness, eating disorders, depression, and student stress with groups of staff and students. He points out that making game shows a regular fixture decreases student dread of these often uncomfortable topics. "They just want to play the game. They don't seem to mind that it is about really uncomfortable things—which is a nice change from just wanting the sessions to be over and sitting in silence. There's nothing worse than a group of people avoiding eye contact for an hour because they're terrified that you'll try to interact with them about *that topic.*"

Soft skills including sexual harassment and diversity training are among the top trained topics. That's at least partially because the failure to learn this information can have severe consequences. You wouldn't want your trainees shutting off at this crucial training time simply because the topic is a little uncomfortable. Game shows can help broach the topic and keep trainees' attention high during this time.

Although both of the instructors in the case study focused on topics that are classified under "soft skills" training, game shows can also be used with particularly difficult material—even rocket science. In fact, some of these types of companies use game shows to train their employees:

- Pharmaceutical companies
- Medical and biological research centers
- Military and government institutions (including training on rocket science)
- Financial service companies

Myth 3: They're Too Difficult to Create and Take Too Much Time to Construct . . . I Don't Have That Kind of Time to Spend Every Week.

Truth: Game shows can be as elaborate as you want to make them or as simple as you need them to be. Software shells can take a lot of the grunt work out of the creation process. In most, all you have to do is type your questions and answers. If you're really pressed for time, there are companies that offer content modules for common training topics; import the questions into your game, and you're ready to go. (See Chapter Sixteen for more information on using game show software.)

If you only have a few minutes, you can use a few sticky notes on tagboard to create a nine-square *Jeopardy!* board or have a short round of *Family Feud*. You can also recycle game show boards or formats to make creation a lot easier the next time.

Sometimes it can take a good chunk of time to create a game show. This is especially true if you're working on a particularly long, involved, or media-heavy game show. One trainer shared that as a rule, it takes three minutes of preparation for every one minute of game show played in the classroom.

We've spent an entire day creating a game show, but we've also created a complete game show for a national sales meeting literally during a fifteen-minute break (we used software in this instance). The bottom line is that it does take time to create a game show, but the results and trainee interaction and participation are definitely worth the effort.

Case Study: Thinking Fast with Game Shows

Susan is the head of training at a large financial institution. After every big group meeting, she conducts a game show to build teamwork and reinforce the points of the meeting. Susan, however, is not always the one leading the meeting so she isn't informed of the content beforehand, and her game shows are often built during five-minute breaks. Despite the somewhat harried conditions, Susan accomplishes her goal to build teamwork and pulls off a polished game show performance every time. "We really love it," says Susan. "The game shows are extremely easy to use, and updates or changes to the games are simple to complete."

It didn't take Susan long to create a game show, but it made a difference that exceeded her time investment. They energized the meetings and related directly to the content at hand.

Myth 4: I Don't Have Time in My Training Session for a Game . . . I Have Too Much Material to Cover.

Truth: Game shows don't have to replace the time you devote to training. Most people have reviews and recap sessions during or after the main training session anyway. This is where game shows can be used as a quick review. Although television game shows last half an hour, yours doesn't have to. Even a five-minute review with a game show can be beneficial to capture trainees' knowledge and ensure that your information is in their heads.

Think about this: when you review with a game show, you gain insight into knowledge gaps that your students may have. Knowing what they know and don't know can help you focus and leverage the time you have remaining in your training session—saving you time overall and helping you achieve your training goals. Because game shows also increase retention, you'll save time in your training session, especially if the upcoming material builds off of the material you're reviewing with the game show.

Case Study: Thank God for Game Shows!

Roger, a Baptist minister, started using game shows with his congregation. He wanted a way to quickly review his sermons in the service and in Sunday school, but he didn't have a lot of time for a big production. "The key to game shows is creativity. They're a very fluid piece, so even for a religious organization, they're very, very flexible. That's been the best thing about it: I can use game shows for any topic at any time. If I want a five-minute review, I can do a five-minute review. If I want a five-minute primer, I can do that too." Roger's congregation has reacted favorably to the game shows: they're more energized throughout the sermon, and they remember more of the details.

A major computer company wanted to use game shows in its training but didn't have a block of time to devote to a game show. Instead of having one long match, the trainer broke the game show into two-minute segments and used them as a refresher to refocus the trainees. The sustained competition kept the energy level high the entire time, and the business didn't have to sacrifice any training time.

Whether in a church or in a large company, game shows are extremely flexible if you don't get hung up on how they're "supposed" to be played. Breaking up a game show into small segments can be useful, even in a training session that is tight on time.

We'll list some tips on deciding how long your game should be later in this book. Remember that just because a game show is short doesn't mean that it can't be effective. Even a quick preview, review, or energizer is good for increasing your audiences' attention and energy—as well as knowledge.

Myth 5: Game Shows Don't Fit the Company Culture . . . We Just Don't DO That Kind of Thing Here.

Truth: We've been raised to believe that because training is serious, training methods must be serious. Training IS serious, and that's why it is so important to present information in a way that people will remember and use. Sometimes that means using unconventional methods in a conventional environment. Game shows don't have to be tacky, loud, or over-the-top; they can be tailored to match your culture and your needs. Something as simple as changing the description or name can affect the reception and perception of a game show. Instead of introducing a game show as a "game," you could call it a "content review challenge."

You may also change the look of your game show to suit your culture or climate. Not every game show has to have an eye-popping game board, confetti, glitter, and streamers. You may want to try a game board with muted tones, company colors, or a whiteboard. Some game shows are naturally more glitzy than others. You may want to avoid playing a bright *Jeopardy!* game and instead go with a more "corporate" feeling *Who Wants to Be a Millionaire?*

Game shows are a strategic tool in both formal and informal environments. You'd be surprised how much people in ties and three-piece suits yell, cheer, and jump about when a game is introduced into their training session.

Case Study: Culture Change

A trainer from a building company relates the story of the first time she used a game show in her training.

The Saturday morning of the class was "very nerve-racking." The superintendents (more than forty of them) were not at all happy to be in the training center for a class, especially not on a Saturday morning.

"How they would receive the *Millionaire*-style game show was starting to worry me," said the trainer.

When it came time for the review, the trainer divided the room into two sections, turned on her computer, and explained the instructions of the game show.

"They appeared very disgusted that I would even suggest such a thing," said the trainer, "but since their executive vice president was in the room, they were a captive audience."

The game started off fairly calmly and then progressed into a real "World-Wide Wrestling Federation–like" match-up.

"They were standing in the chairs, yelling the answers, and even trying to cheat, if you can imagine that!" explains the trainer. "I had to chide the executive vice president for using code words to give his teammates the answers. The losing team demanded a rematch."

The trainees played the game twice and in the end gave it rave reviews.

"They all asked if they could meet again next quarter for another challenge," said the trainer. "The transformation was amazing. To this day when I see any of those guys, they all want to come to training if we can play that game again. Who would have thought that would happen in a company like this?"

Although the trainees were skeptical at first, the excitement and effectiveness of the game show quickly won them over.

In fact, many companies that are using game shows in training are some that one would expect to have the most resistance—for example:

- Department of Defense (including the Air Force, Marines, Army, and Navy)

- Bureau of Prisons

- Pharmaceutical companies like Johnson & Johnson, Pfizer, Merck, and Biogen

- The Internal Revenue Service and accounting firms like H&R Block, Bank One, and Americredit

- Medical institutions like St. Jude Children's Hospital, Johns Hopkins Hospital, the Mayo Clinic, and Beth Israel Medical Center

- Insurance companies like Blue Cross Blue Shield, American Family Insurance, New York Life Insurance, and Farmer's Insurance

- Construction and building companies like ERC Properties

- Automotive, travel, and lodging industries like Starwood Hotels, Toyota, General Motors, and Saturn

Another objection frequently heard is, "I don't think that I could be a game show host." We won't dispel this myth here (and it is a myth—anyone can be a game show host). But in Part Four of this book on conducting a game show, we do away with the myth and provide more information on being an effective trainer-host.

Frequently Asked Questions

While we're giving you straight answers to some of the most commonly held myths and misconceptions, we would also like to present some of the most frequently asked questions about game shows.

Questions	Answers
Is there a time of day that's best to play game shows?	There's no right time of day to play a game show. They can be played at any point during the training session. Where you place your game show should depend on the content of your training session. However, if you wish to use the game show to energize your audience, key points to play are early in the morning, right after lunch, and fifteen to twenty minutes before the end of a training session.

Questions	Answers
Is there any instance when a game show wouldn't be appropriate?	Game shows can be adapted to most situations and content, including sensitive and serious material. Nevertheless, sometimes good taste dictates that a game show not be used. Generally these are times when the "security" of your trainees is threatened (perhaps because of potential layoffs, a death in the company, or major company upsets).
Is it possible to play a game show without a host?	It is possible to play a game show without the host or trainer. In these instances, game show software programs would be played on individual or team computers in a self-directed training format.
Do game shows continue to be as effective after I've used them several times and even with the same class?	Every game show we've ever played has been different—even if it's the same content with the same trainees. Although you do not want to repeat the same content with the same trainees more than twice, there is a dynamic human element in game shows that changes each time you play. A different team may win, different strategies are employed, and trainees view the game differently each time. Repetition is also one of the most effective ways to ensure that trainees retain the maximum amount of information.

Questions	Answers
If I have a bad game show experience, should I bother bringing them up again?	Of course! We've found that most "bad" game show experiences can be chalked up to a lack of game show experience. Most problems within your game show can be fixed once you know what they are. Review the troubleshooting guide in Chapter Seventeen for more information on tweaking your game show.

Now that we've dispelled the myths and misconceptions surrounding game shows and answered some of the most frequently asked questions, it's time to move on to the most challenging and (some would say) the most fun part of training game shows: game show selection, customization, and creation.

Part II

Designing a Game Show for Learning

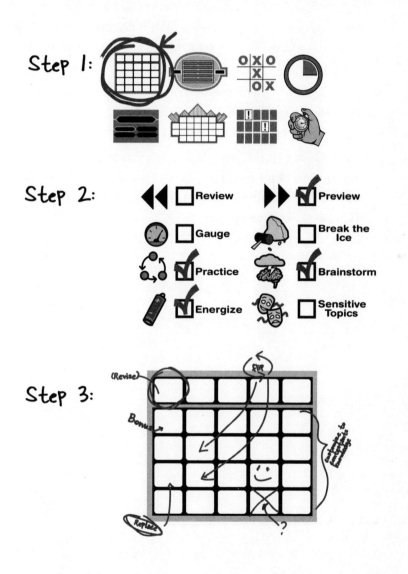

The chapters in Part Two walk you through the process of selecting and designing your own game show so that it is a useful tool that you feel comfortable calling your own. This process contains three easy steps:

Step 1: Review game show choices. We'll discuss eight popular game show formats and their strengths and limitations (Chapter Four).

Step 2: Match the game show to your content and objectives. How you select your game show is dependent on your objectives and the content you want to cover (Chapter Five).

Step 3: Customize the game show to suit your needs. We'll show you how to tailor the game show to suit your outcomes and objectives, including customizing the rules and game play (Chapters Six through Eight).

Chapter 4

Catalogue of Game Shows

In This Chapter, You Will:

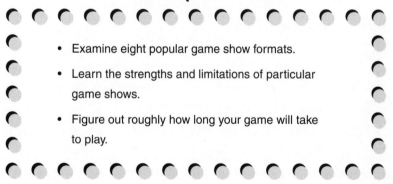

- Examine eight popular game show formats.
- Learn the strengths and limitations of particular game shows.
- Figure out roughly how long your game will take to play.

W e're going to look at popular game shows and see how they can be played in a classroom scenario. Although we mention only the more popular and familiar game shows, your training game show doesn't have to look like any of these; it can be something completely of your own creation. We chose these eight games not only because they are among the most popular (and therefore have a shorter learning curve), but also because they cover the full spectrum of any training need or scenario. These games are:

- *Jeopardy!*

- *Family Feud*

- *Tic-Tac-Dough*

- *Beat the Clock*

- *Wheel of Fortune*

- *Concentration*

- *Who Wants to Be a Millionaire?*

- *College Bowl*

We will be referring to these eight games throughout the book. For each game, we'll define:

Descriptions and rules: This is a summary of how the game show is typically played and should be considered a springboard to start designing your own game show.*

Running time: This is the approximate range of time to play a typical match. This range will change based on your content and does not include the time to introduce the game and set up the teams.

*Descriptions of game shows are based on *The Encyclopedia of TV Game Shows*, by D. Schwartz, S. Ryan, and F. Wostbrock. New York: Checkmark Books, 1999.

Strengths and limitations: With each game show there are strengths and limitations depending on the situation and material. We list the strengths and limitations to give you a selection guide of the best game shows for your needs. Note that almost all limitations listed can be overcome by modifying elements or the rules of the game. (See Chapter Six for suggestions.)

Jeopardy!

Description

One of television's most popular and enduring game shows, *Jeopardy!* is a fast-paced game that is great for reviewing facts.

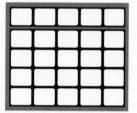

It begins with a *Jeopardy!* round—typically consisting of six categories with five questions each. The questions are worth a varying number of points—traditionally money values from $200 to $1,000. The difficulty level of the question usually coincides with the increasing point values.

Contestants compete for points or money by first selecting a category and point value. When the question (in the form of an answer) is revealed, teams have an allotted time period to "ring in" to answer the question. The first contestant to ring in answers the question in the form of a question; for example, if the answer is, "This is the largest continent in the world," the contestant would pose the question: "What is Asia?" If the contestant answers correctly, he or she wins the point value of the question and gets to select the next category and point value. If the contestant is incorrect, he or she loses the point value indicated, and the other contestants have an opportunity to ring in and answer the question. If no contestant answers the question correctly or the time runs out before anyone rings in, the answer is revealed, and the last person to answer a question correctly gets to select the next category and point value.

Hidden behind the questions is one special "bonus question" that can be answered only by the contestant who selected that question. That person can wager all or part of his or her accumulated points. The amount wagered will be added to the contestant's total score if the response is correct and subtracted if the response is incorrect. No other contestants are allowed to ring in or to answer the bonus question if the response is incorrect.

There is typically a second round called "double *Jeopardy!*" where there are six different categories with five questions for each—but with their point values doubled (traditionally from $400 to $2,000). In this round there are two bonus questions.

The game ends with a "final question" where all the contestants wager points from their accumulated score based on a category heading. After they wager their points, the question is revealed. They are then given time (typically one to two minutes) to write down their answer to the question. If they answer correctly, the points they wagered are added to their score; otherwise, they are deducted. The contestant with the highest accumulated score wins the game.

Running Time per Match

Five to fifteen minutes. This depends on the number of questions per match. You should figure five minutes would clear a nine-question board (three categories times three questions). Fifteen minutes will clear a twenty-five-question match. A typical game contains two matches. A game always take more time if you elaborate on content during the game.

Strengths

- Very familiar game with easy-to-understand rules

- Can display a large number of questions in a short period of time

- Allows grouping questions into categories and assigning different levels of difficulty

- Increasing point values in higher matches makes it possible for teams in last place to catch up

- Fast paced—good energizer

Limitations

- The game penalizes those who are slow readers or have slow recall.

- One of the more difficult games to create and administer without software.

- The rapid-fire question-response nature of this game limits collaboration among teams.

- Not good for questions with highly involved answers or complex scenarios that use role playing.

Family Feud

Description

The television version of *Family Feud* challenges contestants to guess the top answers from a survey of a hundred adults. For example, "Name a condiment you put on a hamburger," might have the most popular  answers of ketchup (50 answers), then mustard (26 answers), and then pickles (24 answers). There can be a varying number of responses to a question—typically from three to seven.

Two teams of five people (in the original show, they were family members) play the game, facing off against each other to guess the top answers. First, a face-off between one contestant from each team starts the round. Whoever rings in first gets first crack at guessing an answer. If the response is listed on the board, this person must wait for the other team's contestant to respond. The contestant with the higher response is given a choice whether to play or pass to the other team.

The team that plays the questions takes turns guessing the remaining answers, going down their row of teammates until they uncover all answers, or get three strikes. Each answer has a percentage of responses (the number of people surveyed who gave that answer); when they uncover a response, a team earns that amount of points. If the team gives three incorrect answers—giving them "strikes"—the members must forfeit play to the other team. At that point, the other team will get a chance to "steal" points by guessing one remaining answer. If they get one answer on the board, they win the other team's points. If not, the first team keeps their points.

The team with the most points after a round (five to seven questions) wins. Or the team with the most points after a certain number of questions (typically five to seven) goes on to the fast money bonus round. In the bonus round, two members from the winning team are selected to play. The first member is given fifteen seconds to uncover the top answers to five different survey questions. The second member is then brought out and given twenty seconds to answer the same questions—with the goal of getting to 200 points total.

For training purposes, you will either want to eliminate the bonus round completely or play it as an additional round with two people from opposing teams. Each team member would answer the bonus questions separately from one another. The team member with the overall higher score after answering the bonus round would either receive all the points from the bonus round to add to the total score or win automatically (depending on how you choose to set up the game).

Running Time per Match

Allow three minutes per question. A typical round has five to seven questions for a fifteen- to twenty-minute game. A bonus round typically takes a minute or less.

Strengths

- The single-question multiple answer format allows a variety of questions not available in the other games—for example: "Name the top five benefits of product X," "List the four steps to processing a loan," "Name the five Great Lakes," or "What six items must be included in placing an order?"

- Allows the trainer to focus on the same question for an extended period of time in order to elaborate on each correct or incorrect answer.

- Encourages individual responses as well as collaboration within the teams.

- Good for building interest or curiosity around new content. For instance, if you were conducting a training session on safety, you could ask the contestants to guess the top five workplace hazards. This opens up discussion and allows them to compare their preconceptions to the reality of the situation.

- This format doesn't penalize trainees who can't read or react quickly.

- The team not answering the questions must stay engaged in the game in case they have the opportunity to "steal" the points.

Limitations

- Only two teams can play at a time, limiting the number of people who can play the game the traditional way.

- Cannot be used with single-answer or multiple-choice questions.

- A single question takes more time to answer than questions in other games.

Tic-Tac-Dough

Description

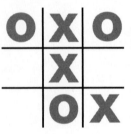

Tic-Tac-Dough is based on the internationally popular children's game known as Tic-Tac-Toe. On the game show version, there are two teams—the X team and the O team.

The teams are shown a 3-by-3 grid, with each of the nine boxes labeled with a different category or number. A coin toss (or other type of random selection) takes place to determine a starting team. The teams then take turns selecting a square from the grid to play. Each square has an associated point value.

When the team selects the square, they must answer a question in order to claim that square for the team. If they answer the question correctly, they leave their respective X or O in the square, and the points are added to the game's jackpot. If they answer the question incorrectly, the square is left blank and no points are added (if it is selected again, there will be a new question to answer). Play passes back and forth between the two teams.

The goal of the round is for a team to get three of its symbols (X or O, respectively) in a row horizontally, diagonally, or vertically on the grid. If the game is a "cat's game" (no team gets three in a row), the team with more symbols on the board is awarded the points. The winning team gets the jackpot that has been accumulating from both teams' efforts.

Multiple rounds can be played; in each round, the category types are randomly placed in different locations on the grid. The winner is the team that has accumulated the most points from all the respective rounds.

Running Time per Match

Between three and nine minutes per round, depending on how much time you'd like to allot to answer questions and the complexity of your questions and answers.

Strengths

- *Tic-Tac-Dough* is typically a familiar game with easy-to-understand rules.

- Easy to administer, with no ringing in required.

- Can be used for a variety of questions—almost any kind you would want, including short answer, essay and role-play, or physical challenge.

- Perfect for team collaboration.

- Easy to set up teams; simply divide the room in half.

Limitations

- Only two teams can play at a time.

- Game play can be redundant or simplistic.

- Doesn't have the flashiness of some of the other games.

- The team to go first in *Tic-Tac-Dough* can have a huge strategic advantage over the other team in terms of arranging their Xs or Os in a row.

Beat the Clock

Description

 This fast-paced game show involves team members working together to successfully achieve physical challenges. The teams were originally selected at random from the television audience. Examples of the challenges in the TV show (long since off the air) include one team member throwing raw eggs to his teammate across the room—who in turn tried to catch them in a mixing bowl. Hilarity and sloppiness ensued. The stunts had to be completed in a preset period of time for the team to earn points. In the end, the team with more accumulated points won the game.

Naturally, there are problems duplicating this concept in the training room—like those pesky standards of cleanliness and civility (plus concerns of lawsuits if someone is hit in the eye with an egg)—not to mention that there is little legitimate reason for egg throwing in training. We do, however, like the idea of having audience members move around and work together to perform stunts.

The "stunts" you incorporate for the training space can be both physical and intellectual. Here are some examples of physical stunts:

- Stock a grocery shelf according to the company's new plan-o-gram (shelf-stocking product layout).

- Refill the receipt tape on a cash register.

- Correctly apply a splint to a "broken leg."

Examples of intellectual challenges include the following:

- Write down at least ten benefits of a new product on a flip chart in sixty seconds.

- Locate and correct ten grammatical errors in a paragraph.

- Attach names to the new organizational chart.

The original *Beat the Clock* had a $100 clock round, a $200 clock round, and a jackpot round, in which a designated player would try to unscramble a phrase or quotation for extra points. Throughout the rounds, there were also particularly difficult bonus stunts, whose value increased as other teams missed completing the stunt. (For example, the stunt started out with a value of $100 and increased by $100 each time a team couldn't do the stunt.)

 Running Time per Match

This is completely up to you—it depends on how many challenges you want to include. It's probably good to figure about five minutes per challenge, plus time to debrief (and clean up as necessary).

Strengths

- This is a great energizer that can be introduced throughout a class.

- Requires teamwork to be successful.

- Allows one team to deal with a question or a challenge for an extended length of time.

- A great audience game. The physical activities can be fun to watch as well as participate in.

Limitations

- This is not the best format for fact-based questions.

- Involving both teams at once can be difficult without a second facilitator.

- This is a more difficult game than the others to administer. The very nature of having the physical stunts takes more time to set up, execute, and clean up afterward.

Wheel of Fortune

Description

Wheel of Fortune is based loosely on the playground Hangman word game, where players try to figure out a hidden word or phrase by guessing letters that may be in the phrase. In *Wheel of Fortune,* you add a wheel (surprise!) that each contestant must spin before guessing a letter. The wheel has point values that indicate how much each correct letter is worth. It also has penalties dispersed around the board such as "Lose a Turn" and "Bankrupt." "Bankrupt" will remove any points that the contestant may have in the bank. After a player guesses a letter correctly, it is revealed on the master board that contains a hidden phrase. A player will continue to spin and earn points until losing a turn or making an incorrect guess—in which case the next player gets a chance to play.

Players continue to take turns, building up points in their bank and revealing letters until a contestant correctly guesses the secret word or phrase and wins all the points in their bank.

While players earn points for guessing consonants correctly, they have to "buy" vowels (in the TV show, the vowels cost $250 a piece) by giving up a predesignated portion of their score.

To make this a training game show, have the contestants correctly answer a question at the beginning of their turn in order for them to be able to spin the wheel. They either answer just one question and then have unlimited spinning privileges, or they may have to answer a question before each spin of the wheel.

Running Time per Match

Allot three to eight minutes per round. Figure in three minutes if the word puzzle is relatively simple and the contestants answer few questions, or assume closer to eight minutes if the word puzzle is difficult and contestants answer questions before every spin.

Strengths

- Fun, popular game that is a great energizer.

- You can make the word puzzle relevant to your training by making it a phrase or word that describes the goal of training or an important directive.

- You can play the game without asking questions to serve as a midtraining energizer.

- As with *Tic-Tac-Dough*, you can ask a variety of questions, including open-ended ones, which will give the contestants more time to perform critical thinking tactics.

Limitations

- Unlike other types of games that rely solely on the skill and knowledge of the trainees, this game introduces an element of chance (the wheel). This can be negative reinforcement if someone answers a question correctly and then goes "bankrupt." (This also might inspire a few "that's not fair" statements, but typically people understand this as part of the game and take a bad spin in good humor.)

- Spinning the wheel and solving the puzzle can be a distraction from the actual content if the questions are not emphasized over solving the word puzzle.

- Experienced *Wheel of Fortune* contestants may run away with the game before other contestants get a chance to play if they are allowed to keep guessing letters until they guess incorrectly.

Concentration

Description

 On the original *Concentration* television show, contestants tried to solve a rebus (a sentence or phrase composed of pictures) that lay beneath thirty numbered panels. Two contestants would face off, each taking turns. During their turn, a contestant would select two panels, revealing a hidden prize under each. If the two prizes matched, the portion of the rebus that lies beneath would be revealed and the contestant could win the prize displayed on the panels by solving the rebus. The contestant could solve the rebus if enough tiles were revealed to enable the person to do so; otherwise the contestant continued to select two more panels. A player loses control of the board whenever the two panels selected do not have matching prizes. Control passes back and forth between the players until one solves the rebus. The player who solves the rebus is declared champion and wins all the prizes they collected through-out the game.

For training purposes, the pairs of prizes on the panels can be a hidden question-and-answer set. For instance, one card could be, "This is the form number for filling out an expense report." The other card—the match—would be "Form C-48."

You may choose to leave out the rebus section and declare the team with the most matching sets the winner.

 Running Time per Match

Between eight and ten minutes depending on the complexity of the rebus and the number of matching pairs.

Strengths

- This is especially effective for languages. Trainees can try to match the foreign word or acronym with its English or lengthened equivalent. (You can award extra points by allowing the contestant to use the word in a sentence.)

- This is good for mathematical and short equation questions.

- Can effectively teach feature and benefit pairings.

- Each team has to pay attention to the game at all times to see which tiles the other team has uncovered.

- A team can often remember more than an individual could alone. The collaboration involved in concentration provides the opportunity for a team to remember the location of squares better than an individual could.

Limitations

- Success isn't based solely on content knowledge. *Concentration* by its very nature requires memory.

- Contestants have to remember where matching tiles are located.

- There may be times when contestants can get a matching question and answer without knowing that they match (random chance). One way to deal with this is to ask follow-up questions after every correct match to make sure that contestants understand the material.

- This can be hard to implement. You have to keep flipping around cards and have to think of a picture or rebus to put in back of the cards.

- Rebuses are complex and may take practice in order to solve quickly. It's also difficult to create a unique or relevant rebus. The rebus limitation can be lessened somewhat by simply putting a word or phrase (in large type, different fonts, or "ransom letter" style) behind the squares.

Who Wants to Be a Millionaire?

Description

The way that the *Millionaire* game is played on TV, ten contestants first compete for the chance to play the game in the "hot seat" by answering a sequencing question. The first contestant to answer the question in the correct order plays the game.

In the *Millionaire* game, the single contestant will answer a series (or "ladder") of multiple-choice questions that increase in both difficulty and point value. There is no time limit on answering the questions. At this point, the game is based on suspense, not speed. The multiple-choice questions are given to the contestant before he or she decides whether to play on. If the trainee is unable to answer a question, there are three "lifelines" for help that a contestant may use once per variation within a game: "Ask the audience," where the audience is polled to figure out what they think the answer is; "50–50," where the computer randomly takes away half of the incorrect multiple-choice options; and "Phone a friend," where the contestant can call a friend or content expert to see if he or she can give the answer within thirty seconds. At any time during the game, a contestant who decides he or she is unable to answer a question—even with the lifeline options—can walk away with a base level amount of points. If the contestant answers a question incorrectly, he or she loses the points.

In a classroom setting, two teams compete against each other, alternating answers to see which can get the higher level of points and difficulty.

Running Time per Match

Between four minutes and an hour, depending on the number of levels, lifelines, and the time allotted for each question.

Strengths

- This can be used with a variety of questions, allowing teams to collaborate, brainstorm, and think about the questions.

- *Millionaire* is flexible in terms of the allotted playing time and how many people can play, plus the traditional game allows an unlimited time to answer questions.

- Doesn't require ring-in from any team.

- Hints and clues jog the contestants' memories and give them a deeper understanding of the material.

Limitations

- Questions should be created with increasing difficulty as contestants travel up the ladder.

- Teams don't compete to answer the same questions, so it can get tedious for the nonplaying team during the other team's turn.

- Without time limits, it can take a long time to play and will generate less energy than some of the other games.

College Bowl

Description

In a *College Bowl* game, there are two teams with four contestants each. The teams compete to answer two types of questions: ring-in questions (also called toss-up questions) and extra-credit questions (or bonus questions). Each toss-up has an associated bonus question, usually worth more points than its toss-up question. A delegate from each team is selected to face off in the toss-up question. The contestant who answers a toss-up question correctly earns the opportunity for the team to earn additional points by answering the bonus question. Incorrect answers for either question type are not penalized.

The game typically ends with a Speed Round, where any team can ring in and answer questions within a sixty-second time period.

The winning team is the one with the higher point total at the end of the second round.

Running Time per Match

A typical match lasts fifteen to twenty-five minutes depending on the number of bonus questions in the game and the time allotted for each question.

Strengths

- Bonus questions allow trainers to explore a topic in depth.

- Encourages both individual initiative and team collaboration.

- A large variety of question formats can be used.

Limitations

- This format can penalize trainees who can't read or react quickly.

- If played in the traditional way (where the team that answers toss-up questions correctly is given the exclusive opportunity to answer the bonus question on the same topic), one team can "run away" with the game.

- The game format is not as well known as some of the others and may take longer to explain.

All of the game shows profiled here have been used with tremendous success in the training classroom, and all lend themselves to full customization.

Now that you know some of the most popular game shows and why they work in a training scenario, it's time to select which game show you would like to use based on what you want to accomplish using the show.

Chapter 5

Selecting the Right Game
for Your Purpose

In This Chapter, You Will:

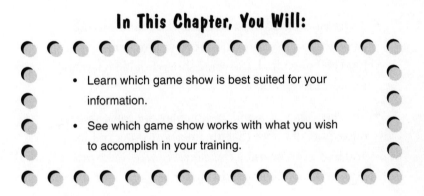

- Learn which game show is best suited for your information.
- See which game show works with what you wish to accomplish in your training.

In this chapter, we'll help you figure out which game shows fit your objectives. We'll look at matching your content with a game show and which format will work best for your desired results.

Our suggestions are based on what we've found works. We are constantly surprised by the different applications trainers find for game shows, and we're sure that you'll have your own creative ideas that don't necessarily fit neatly into one of our categories. This section will make a good jumping-off point for your own ideas. Keep in mind that with the variety in game show formats and infinite ways of modifying each game's rules, it's safe to say that a game show can be created to suit any type of training.

Think about your objective. Is it:

- *To review content?* Most trainers we've talked to use game shows for information review. Once the content has been presented, the game show should review and reinforce that content.

- *To gauge comprehension?* As you play the game show, make note of topics that are unclear to your trainees. You may even be using the game show as a test to see how well they do know the material.

- *To practice and apply skills?* You want trainees to demonstrate and practice your content within the game show.

- *To energize the classroom?* You would like the game show to serve as a pick-me-up and energizer. It may or may not have questions that directly relate to the content of your training.

- *To preview content?* You are about to start a topic and want to introduce the basic theme or elements with a game show to generate interest and curiosity.

- *To introduce sensitive topics?* You know that you're going to have some touchy material in your training and would like to use a game show to relieve tension and make a smooth transition to a discussion.

- *To break the ice?* Your trainees and you have just met each other or have just sat down in the training space. You would like to start a base of teamwork and camaraderie while letting the trainees get to know each other (and you!).

- *To brainstorm?* Your trainees need to come up with solutions, learn brainstorming strategies, or find their own creative answers to a problem. Game shows would be used to generate new ideas and thinking.

Game Shows for Content Review

If you want to do a simple review to go through previously covered information, practically any game show will work. However, some are better suited to the different types of content you may have.

Reviewing Facts and Figures

A fact or figure would include laws, policies, product specifications, plain data, "trivia," or research results. Almost anything that is considered "book knowledge" is a fact or a figure.

If you have a lot of fact-related information that you want to review, the *Jeopardy!* and *College Bowl* formats have the advantage of delivering the greatest amount of content in the shortest period of time. With *Jeopardy!* you can play through more than fifty questions in just thirty minutes—including time to elaborate on select questions. The *Millionaire*, *Tic-Tac-Dough*, and *Wheel of Fortune* game show formats work as well, but do not have the same rapid-style delivery of *Jeopardy!* or *College Bowl*.

The *Family Feud* format works for reviewing facts only if the facts have multiple answers—for example, "Name the presidents carved in Mount Rushmore" or "Name the seven continents."

Reviewing Processes and Procedures

Processes and procedures include auditing, strategy, formulation, assembly, bank telling, and legal procedures. Anything that has multiple steps is a process or procedure.

Generally this type of information review requires a little more time to think and often a longer answer time. If the process is complex, you may want team members to collaborate before developing an answer.

Because you want more allotted time to discuss and answer questions, games that do not require ringing in, like the *Who Wants to Be a Millionaire?*, *Tic-Tac-Dough*, and *Wheel of Fortune* game formats are suited for processes and procedure review. These formats provide an opportunity to collaborate and formulate an answer—as well as allowing extra time for performing or listing an answer. *Beat the Clock* can be used to demonstrate a process or procedure if the timers are adjusted to allow for "think time" before contestants must ring in.

If you would like to use a *Jeopardy!* format, allow more time for players to read and view the question before requiring them to ring in. This will give them the opportunity to search their brains before attempting to answer the question. You also have the option to embed the most complex process-oriented questions under a bonus question or as a final question (neither of which requires ringing in).

The *Family Feud* game show format excels when you want to review processes or procedures that have multiple steps. Examples might be, "Name the four steps to validate a PS4 contract" or "Name the three parts of a 104B legal contract."

Reviewing Languages

Languages include acronyms, foreign languages, business, and professional jargon.

Languages are one area where a *Concentration* game format is most useful. Participants match the foreign word or phrase with its

English counterpart. Any of the other game show formats work effectively with language review—even a *Family Feud* type of game. In fact, using questions and answers (even if they are just trivia-type questions) in a foreign language is a good way for students to practice that language. They are engaged and invested in answering the question correctly and can see the new language used in context.

Game Shows to Gauge Comprehension

As with games to review content, practically any game can be used to gauge the comprehension of your students. Which game you use depends on what you are trying to gauge: recall or recognition.

If you're gauging recall, you'll want to measure a trainee's understanding of the material. In this case use games that accommodate open-ended or essay questions or role play, or allow more time for trainees to answer, discuss, and apply particular principles. Games that are best for gauging recall are *Tic-Tac-Dough* and *Who Wants to Be a Millionaire?*

If you're gauging recognition, you'll want to determine a trainee's memory of the material. In this case, use more rapid-fire games that require trainees to think quickly and react almost automatically. Games that are best for gauging recognition are *Jeopardy!*, *Wheel of Fortune*, and *College Bowl*.

Game Shows to Practice and Apply Skills

Practicing and applying skills in a training game show requires more time to set up a question or scenario and more time to answer or demonstrate. Therefore, games that are fast-paced like *Jeopardy!* are best left for fact-based questions that are more receptive to quick answers.

Tic-Tac-Dough, Beat the Clock, Wheel of Fortune, and *Who Wants to Be a Millionaire?* game formats all work well, because the trainer has the freedom to take time to set up a scenario or a task. Consequently the trainees also have more time to demonstrate their skill or answer. Keep in mind these points:

- In cases where answers that involve role play are included, correctness is not always black-and-white. Judgments have to be made based on the completeness or accuracy of the answer.

- When participants are practicing and applying skills, it is often necessary to elaborate and debrief. Make sure to build in time to do so.

Game Shows to Energize the Classroom

When you want to wake up the room or add a little life to the middle of a training session, almost any game show format will work as long as it is fast-paced and relatively short. Because of their longer playing time, *Tic-Tac-Dough*, *Concentration*, and *Wheel of Fortune* are formats to stay away from. Otherwise a *Jeopardy!* format is an obvious choice because of the rapid question-and-answer format, as are *Family Feud*, *Concentration*, *Beat the Clock*, and *College Bowl*.

Game Shows to Preview Content

Game shows are highly effective when used to preview information and get trainees thinking about content. If you want to generate curiosity around a topic, you'll want them to compare their assumptions and preexisting opinions with reality to get a handle on what they know or don't know about a subject. The best way to do this is to keep the games short and noncompetitive. After all, you're assuming that your trainees have little understanding of the material. Having an all-out competition won't reflect their knowledge in the best light and may make them feel intimidated.

When the odds of answering questions correctly are lower, games like *Jeopardy!* that penalize wrong answers are not the best choices. However, if you have your heart set on *Jeopardy!* use no more than a three-by-three grid—it's not much fun watching a game show if all the scores are in the negative!

The game show that we've found to be the most effective to preview content is *Family Feud*. In this game, you can ask open-ended questions to reveal trainees' assumptions and opinions. For example, you could ask, "Name the top five customer technical complaints for the Zoom-4 processor." The trainees will start listing the complaints that they think customers may have based on their knowledge or experiences. Although their answers may not match the correct answers on the board, they are thinking along the right track. Comparing what they thought was correct to the right answers will generate some, "Wow, I didn't realize that!" thinking. *Who Wants to Be a Millionaire?* is also a good preview game since there are lifelines that can help trainees through content they don't know.

Another option for preview that can work in the same way as *Family Feud* is *Beat the Clock*. If you are asking, "What internal behaviors cause our customers to take their business elsewhere?" you could have trainees list their answers on an easel or whiteboard, or have them physically act out what they think are the undesirable behaviors. In the end, you would reveal your master list of correct answers and award points for correct answers.

You may be noticing a pattern in previewing: lists. When you're trying to ease trainees into unfamiliar territory or trying to make them aware of their own misconceptions, having them make a list is an effective way to get their thoughts flowing. Often the first thoughts that pop into our minds are very predictable. If you ask just one question with just one answer, you'll get the trainees' first thought. By asking them to list their answers, you'll get them to stretch their thinking to more original ideas.

Game Shows to Introduce Sensitive Topics

Almost any game can be used to introduce a sensitive topic, although *Concentration* is to be avoided for obvious reasons: you wouldn't want to use picture matching in a sexually transmitted disease awareness game for example. The key with sensitive topics is to have a game format that will allow you to elaborate when needed but will keep the game moving at a moderate pace. The trainees should feel at ease with the material and not pressured to delve in at a depth that they aren't comfortable with.

Jeopardy! can be used to preview topics, and the category headings provide extra security for the trainees. They can see what topic or material they'll be getting into before they are presented with a question. *Family Feud* is also a good game, since it can open up a conversation about a particular topic in a lighthearted manner. *Who Wants to Be a Millionaire?* and *College Bowl* are effective for sensitive topics because they allow you to control the time for answering more tightly than some other games.

Game Shows to Break the Ice

Game shows used specifically to break the ice are much like game shows to energize the classroom. In both instances, stick with fast-paced games; however, when you want to break the ice, games should have a stronger focus on collaboration. A short *Jeopardy!* game that emphasizes teamwork works well, as does *Family Feud*.

Beat the Clock can be particularly effective since the entire team is physically participating. There's no chance for someone to feel singled out in an activity or put on the spot for a question.

Game Shows to Brainstorm

Game shows for brainstorming allow you to extend the answer times to let groups or individuals collaborate, and that can work without having a set right answer. *Family Feud* works for brainstorming because you are asking groups to generate multiple answers. Instead of going down the row and having individuals answer a question, have the team brainstorm a whole list and give their top answers. You may then discuss what they didn't list as their top answers. *Tic-Tac-Dough, Who Wants to Be a Millionaire?,* and *Beat the Clock* also work well since you can be flexible about which answers are "right" and which are "wrong."

If you want to use games to brainstorm, you may want to consider modifying the scoring so that trainees can be awarded partial credit.

Game Shows That Fit Your Purpose

Table 5.1 summarizes what we've just discussed in this chapter. Almost any game can work for any content. By fixing and changing the game show's rules, you can use most games for any purpose, as we'll show you in the next chapter.

Table 5.1. Selecting a Game Show

	Review	Gauge Comprehension	Practice and Apply Skills	Energize the Classroom	Preview Content	Introduce Sensitive Topics	Break the Ice	Brainstorm
Jeopardy!	X	X		X		X	X	
Family Feud	X			X	X	X	X	X
Tic-Tac-Dough	X	X	X					X
Beat the Clock	X		X	X	X		X	X
Wheel of Fortune	X	X	X					
Concentration	X			X				
Who Wants to Be a Millionaire?	X	X	X		X	X		X
College Bowl	X	X		X		X		

Chapter 6

Customizing Your Game Show

In This Chapter, You Will:

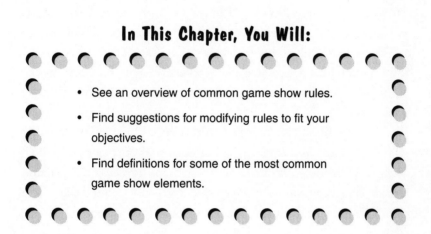

- See an overview of common game show rules.
- Find suggestions for modifying rules to fit your objectives.
- Find definitions for some of the most common game show elements.

We can't stress this enough: *you* make the rules. You don't have to—nor should you—follow all the rules as they are on TV. Make sure that you communicate your rules ahead of time and that the rules lead to an effective learning experience for your trainees. Always explain the rules to your trainees before the game show starts—even if you think they know how the game works. For example, everyone "knows" that in *Jeopardy!* on TV, you must answer in the form of a question. Most trainers we have observed have left out this rule—a "what is . . ." thrown in doesn't really help trainees retain more knowledge and can detract from the game play. However, this may become a point of contention if you don't explain that trainees *don't* have to answer in the form of a question.

Every game has to have clearly defined and established rules. They define how the game is played (very obvious, but very important), give all players an equal opportunity to win, and make you look good.

How do rules make the trainer look good? Imagine that you're playing a game and something happens that may not be "legal" within the parameters of the rules—perhaps trainees on one team decide that they can use their notes. If it is not defined that they can't use notes and you are uncertain about it, you allow it to pass. Then another trainee who really wants to win—you know the type: loud, competitive, and unyielding—brings it up later in the game. Suddenly you're confronted with either going back on your initial decision and acting involuntarily as if you're favoring one team over another or, worse, looking as if you don't have control of the situation. Most of the unproductive conflict between teams occurs because of unclear rules. Established rules are a good way for you to be able to stick to your guns without looking like the bad guy.

 Dos and Don'ts About Rules

Do: Review the rules. Even if you think the game is well known, someone may need a refresher or be out of the loop.

Don't: Assume that everyone knows the rules to even the most common of games. If participants don't know how to play the game, they'll disengage quickly.

Do: Shape the rules to fit your needs and purpose—even if they're not the rules to the original game.

Don't: Shoot for the Nobel Prize in complicated instructions. If your participants don't understand the game, either they won't fully immerse themselves in the game show or your training session will be subject to a large amount of whining. You want the focus to be the game *play*, not *how* the game is played.

Do: Post the rules. Posting the rules (or handing out rule cards like the ones on the CD in this book) keeps the rules fresh in players' minds (and your own as well). You won't have to stop and reexplain something in the middle of the game if it's in front of everyone.

Don't: Rely on players to remember all the peculiarities of the game show, especially if it's their first time playing. Expect to have to give rule reminders if you don't have a rule handout.

Here are some of the things that you should think about when making your rules.

Ringing In

Things to consider:

- Does the team need to ring in to answer a question?
- How do they ring in?
- How do you know who rings in first?

- When are they allowed to ring in?

- When they ring in, does the host stop reading the question?

- If they ring in early, is there a penalty?

Games that require contestants to ring in can offer a greater level of excitement than those that don't. The contestants need to have hair-trigger reflexes to compete for the opportunity to answer questions. These games also tend to have a higher level of competition, so it's crucial that you have a way to determine which team or contestant rings in first. (In Chapter Sixteen we'll review both high-tech and low-tech solutions for ringing in.)

Timers

Things to consider:

- How long do teams have to read the question?

- How much time can pass without ringing in before the answer is revealed?

- Once a team rings in, how long do they have before they must answer?

- What happens if the time runs out before they start their answer?

- Do they get to finish their answer if the timer goes off after they've started?

- If the end-of-game timer goes off during a question, is the question played out, or is it the definitive end?

Timers are crucial for effective game play. They keep the game play going, keep things "fair," and reduce a lot of headaches for you.

Timers are also one of the easiest elements to change. You can set the read, ring in, and answer timers for as long or short as you would like without having to significantly rearrange your game show or add extraneous rules. Timers can also have the biggest impact on the flow of the game.

There are three main types of timers.

Read Timer

In game shows where contestants have to ring in to answer—like *Jeopardy!*—a read timer is needed. This dictates the time that you allow teams to read the question before they can ring in. This prevents a contestant who just completed a speed reading course from having an unfair advantage. If you are reading the question out loud, it also prevents contestants from interrupting you.

Ring-In Timer

The ring-in timer represents the time that contestants are allotted to ring in or express their desire to answer the question before the question is abandoned. For example, in the television version of *Jeopardy!* if no one rings in after a certain amount of time, a bell rings and the host reveals the answer. This prevents an indefinite amount of time passing in silence if the contestants don't know the answer and keeps the game show moving at a reasonable pace.

Answer Timer

This timer regulates how long a team member has before he or she must begin to answer the question. It is okay for a contestant to continue with an answer after the timer has gone off as long as he or she has a reasonable and credible start. In a game where ring-in is required, this starts as soon as the ring-in occurs. Otherwise this starts after the question is read out loud.

In game shows where a contestant must ring in to answer (*Jeopardy!* for example), keep the answer timer short—around five seconds or so. This will prevent a contestant from ringing in and then spending the next fifteen seconds rereading the question and formulating an answer. A short answer timer will ensure that the player must know the answer before ringing in. If it looks as if the contestant is answering a question nonsensically by saying things like, "Well, that's an interesting question. Many things could be said about that, but where does one start? It reminds me of the time when I was twelve . . ." and otherwise trying to stall while searching for the answer, the game show host has the prerogative to assume the person doesn't know the answer and judge it incorrect when the timer expires. Lest this seem unfair, remember that a short answer timer doesn't mean that a contestant's entire answer has to fit into five seconds; it only means that he or she must have had a reasonable and legitimate start by the time the timer goes off.

In game shows where ring-in is not required, allow as much time as necessary for contestants to give a complete answer. If the questions are fact based, ten seconds is a fairly reasonable answer time. If there are questions that require collaboration within a team, longer role-playing scenarios, or physical stunts, the answer timer can be quite a bit longer.

How Long Should a Game Show Be?

A game show should be long enough to be effective and short enough to leave trainees wanting more. If you're in doubt, make the game shorter rather than longer.

Nothing is worse than having too much of a good thing. Watching a game show go from exciting to too long is like watching your childhood heroes grow older—there's something kind of sad about it. The idea of a game show is to keep trainees motivated and engaged, so staying within a practical length is always best. How long is too long? We suggest that you never have a single game go uninterrupted for longer than seventy-five minutes. If you want to play a longer game show, build in breaks to introduce new contestants, new formats, a new game show, new question formats, or even new topics. Keep in mind that in addition to playing the actual game show, you'll need to account for a brief introduction and debriefing.

If you would like to do a more comprehensive, longer game show, try breaking it up throughout the day. We once hosted a game show at a sales meeting that lasted over ninety minutes. The only reason that it was successful was that we broke it into three matches. One match was played midway through the morning, the other after lunch, and the final at the end of the day. The points accumulated throughout the training session, and the students were attentive in between matches and eager to get back to the game show to catch up or to strengthen their lead.

Seventy-five minutes may sound like a long time, especially if you wanted to use a game show to do a quick energizer. But your game shows don't have to span anywhere near seventy-five minutes. If you want to do an energizer, icebreaker, or preview, a five- to fifteen-minute game show is all you would need or want.

In our experience, training game shows usually run from about thirty to forty-five minutes from introduction to the final question. The equivalent number of rounds or matches for each game is shown in Table 6.1.

Table 6.1.   Game Show Length

Game Show	30 to 45 Minutes Equals . . .
Jeopardy!	Two complete matches of twenty-five questions each
Family Feud	Two matches with seven questions each
Tic-Tac-Dough	Three rounds of nine questions each
Beat the Clock	About six to eight challenges
Wheel of Fortune	Six or seven questions with a final word puzzle
Concentration	Two matches with a medium grid size
Who Wants to Be a Millionaire?	Two teams climbing a fifteen-rung ladder (answering fifteen questions apiece)
College Bowl	Two matches including toss-ups, bonus questions, and a speed round

If your training session is not flexible and you have to limit the game show to a set time frame, decide how long you would like a match to run and stop at the preset time. If you have thirty minutes to play two matches of a *Jeopardy!* game, assume:

Five minutes for the introduction and team selection

Three minutes for the final question

Eleven minutes per match (22 total minutes)

Set a timer, and at the end of eleven minutes, end the match whether all the questions have been cleared or not. Make it clear to your trainees that matches will end after eleven minutes. This way you'll avoid complaints like, "But we're behind and there are three questions left. . . ." You may choose to shorten the introduction and final question times to allot more time to answering the questions, but don't do so at the expense of adequate explanations.

Playing a Multiple Match Game

You don't have to play a game show in a single session. For example, if you have a game show with approximately forty-five minutes of content, breaking it into three fifteen-minute sections spread throughout the day might be a better option. Spreading a game show throughout the day (or even over several days) allows you to intersperse reviews in your session and keeps energy levels high. In between the game show segments, you can switch participating contestants on teams and introduce new content.

If you are going to keep tallying the scores over several game show sessions, be sure to recap the scores, the game rules, and the purpose of the game each time you play the game show.

Tips for Keeping the Longer Game Fresh

A longer game doesn't have to go stale. The key is adding variety into your game show:

- Change the rules from round to round.

- Vary the types of questions (incorporating physical movement when possible).

- Add in essay-style (teams have to write a short essay response to a more complex question) or role-playing questions.

- Use questions to keep the entire audience involved.

- Change the game show.

- If you choose to have many game shows throughout the session, keep them short.

- Break your game into multiple matches.

- Use multimedia in your game show.

The key to keeping your game show lively is change. If contestants are constantly challenged by new elements, they'll have a dynamic game show experience.

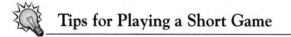

Tips for Playing a Short Game

Not every game has to be an event. It's okay to play a two- or three-minute game show. Sometimes all you need is five minutes to make a big impact on your training. Here are some ideas for keeping things short:

- Don't play the whole game at one time.

- Have one- or two-minute speed rounds throughout the training session.

- Give each team only two questions each game show, and keep a running total of their scores.

- Set a firm time limit, and stop the game show when the timer rings—no matter where you are.

Scoring

A crucial part of game play is the scoring of the game. Point values can inspire competition, determine "winners," and be used to indicate the difficulty level of a question.

Things to consider:

- Can points be deducted, and, if so, under what conditions?

- What is the policy on extra credit? Are there opportunities to earn extra points, and if so, how?

- What are the point values for regular play, extra credit, bonus rounds, and other parts of the game?

- What happens in the case of a tie?

- Is it possible for two teams to get points for the same question?

On TV, the most exciting competitions are when the scores remain close until the very end. The same is true for game shows in your classroom, but for a different reason. You want the teams to always feel that they're in the game and not be discouraged by huge point gaps. If the games have more than one round, increase the point values in later rounds so there is always a chance for the team that is lagging to catch up. You may also use extra credit by inserting bonus questions or even giving teams opportunities to earn extra points by elaborating on questions.

Many opportunities for extra credit use the concept of wagering. For instance, in each of the bonus questions (or "daily doubles") for *Jeopardy!* a contestant may wager part or all of his or her points. The idea is that the greater the risk is, the greater the return can be. Wagers are an effective tool for equalizing scores or so a team can catch up from behind. They can be used in any game show under extra credit or bonus opportunities—not just *Jeopardy!*

Extra credit doesn't always have to be used as an equalizer. You may want to make some material worth more points to emphasize its importance. For example, the "final question" in *Jeopardy!* can be a summary of the material or a concept that you want to drive home.

Points can be used as a penalty as well as a reward. For example, if a team answers incorrectly, you may choose to deduct the number of points that a question was worth from their score. Points may also be deducted for "bad" behavior. (See the Penalties section on the next page.)

When setting point values:

- Keep the values within a tight range for any given round. Typically we see ranges between 100 and 500 points for the first round and 200 and 1,000 points for a subsequent round.

- If a question is more difficult, assign it a higher point value. If it is easier, keep the values lower.

Nevertheless, it is not always necessary to use a point system. When working with very large groups or doing presentations, a point system can be impractical. You may wish to toss out small prizes for each answer that is correct, or you can emphasize the process of playing the game instead of winning teams by praising each individual answer.

A Note About Extra Credit

Extra credit opportunities in the game can be a great chance for teams that are behind to catch up and can be used strategically to test the depth of trainees' knowledge. For instance, a team can get extra credit points by elaborating on the content or answering a more complex follow-up question.

- Use extra credit opportunities sparingly and only as necessary.

- Try to spread extra credit opportunities evenly across the teams.

- Use extra credit at your discretion as a device to help a team that is lagging behind catch up.

- Keep the criteria for distributing extra credit points vague by saying that "extra credit will be available at various times, and some questions will trigger an extra credit opportunity." This way, you are in complete control of the points in the game where extra credit is given.

Penalties

Things to consider:

- How are disputes handled?

- Can points awarded be reversed?

- Is there a "statute of limitations" on awarding or deducting points?

- Are judges' decisions final?

- What is the policy on cheating?

- How do you handle unsportsmanlike behavior?

- What are the penalties for disruptive behavior?

- Can points be deducted, and if so, what are the criteria?

- Can contestants argue with the trainer?

Taking away points from a contestant or team can be an effective way of inhibiting unruly or unsportsmanlike behavior. However, penalties for behavior should be applied sparingly. If you continually need to penalize a team or player, consider asking the culprits to leave the game.

Which types of behaviors should you penalize?

Cheating: Examples are nonplaying members of a team who give answers to their contestants, contestants who look at their notes or other material when they're not supposed to, and spying on another team's collaboration to gain an advantage.

Unsportsmanlike behavior: Examples are booing, mocking, or interfering with the other team's game play; excessively challenging answers; bad-mouthing the game; or being a spoilsport on the team.

Rule violations: This includes violating any of the basic rules laid out before the game. For instance, a person or team may insist on blurting out answers without ringing in, even though you have specified that teams must ring in before answering.

The behaviors that you choose to penalize are up to you—you are both judge and jury. For instance, we've heard of instructors turning a blind eye to contestants who try to look through their materials for answers. Their justification is that the trainees are learning regardless of the "cheating," and they want trainees to get used to using the manuals or training materials. Other trainers may allow rowdy behavior to a certain point (or a certain decibel level). The basic rule for enforcing penalties is that if the infraction is getting in the way of trainees' learning the content, it's time to do something about it.

If you choose to enforce penalties for certain rules, here are some things to consider:

- Be clear about the rules and associated penalties before the game starts.

- Make sure that you treat teams equally and continue to encourage a penalized team in game play.

- Be consistent throughout the game on what you will allow and disallow.

- Consider giving a warning for the first infraction before giving a penalty, particularly if the infraction is excessive rowdiness or equally spirited transgression. However, give only *one* warning per team. Then start enforcing.

- Don't take anything personally, and don't lose your composure. If a team is cheating, they're not trying to make you look like a bad trainer; they just want to win. Gently enforce the penalty without losing your head over it.

In the Penalty Box

How should you penalize teams? Let's look to professional sports for inspiration:

Basketball: The nonoffending team gets several free throws. You can give the nonoffending team a chance to answer a question without the other team's being able to answer, steal, or ring in.

Football: The offending team loses yardage, and the nonoffending team gains yardage. You can deduct points for a penalty or add points to the nonoffending team's score.

Hockey: Offending players have to sit in the penalty box. You can disallow an offending team or player from contributing or answering for a certain amount of time.

Baseball: A player who is behaving badly is out! Offending members can be "traded" or replaced by another team member. Nonoffending teams could pick a member of the offending team to come over to their team.

We particularly like penalties that involve giving the nonoffending team extra points or privileges. In this way, you are rewarding behavior that you would like to reinforce instead of punishing behavior. Always remember not to make the penalty for misbehavior or failure greater than the reward for success or good behavior.

The rules, timers, scoring, and penalties can be adjusted for any game show. You also may want to change specific elements in the game show that are not as rule based but affect how the game is played in a way that is radically different from its TV counterpart. The next chapter provides creative and unique customizations to make to your game show depending on what you wish to accomplish within the game.

Chapter 7

Customizations for Your
Specific Game Show

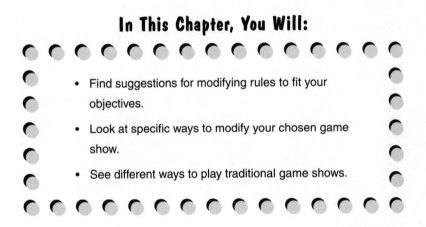

In This Chapter, You Will:

- Find suggestions for modifying rules to fit your objectives.
- Look at specific ways to modify your chosen game show.
- See different ways to play traditional game shows.

Throughout this book, we've been saying that it is often necessary to modify the rules of a game show in order for the game to fit your training. In this chapter, we examine specific ways to adapt the game shows to overcome basic limitations and to better suit your objectives.

Universal Game Show Modifications

These modifications can be applied to almost any game show to suit your training purpose:

If you want to . . .	Then . . .
Eliminate the advantage of faster readers or persons with quick recall	Eliminate the need for ring-in by alternating answer privileges between teams.
	Extend the read-time before contestants are allowed to ring in.
Encourage collaboration	Eliminate the need to ring in.
	Have a long read time so teams can discuss whether they would like to answer a question.
	Increase the number of essay-type or role-play questions.
Reduce anxiety over answering correctly	Remove any penalties for incorrect answers.
Go into depth with your material	After an answer is uncovered, give out extra points if a team member can elaborate on that answer. For example, if the question is about features of a product, extra points can be awarded if the contestant describes the related customer benefit.

Tailoring Your TV Game Show

In the remainder of this chapter, we'll discuss how you can broaden your training results by making a few changes to the established rules of popular game shows.

Jeopardy! Variations

If you want to . . .	Then . . .
Cover more content or lengthen your game	Make a large grid (6×5 or larger).
	Have several matches or rounds.
Shorten your game	Use a small grid (3×3).
	Break the game into several small segments. Don't cover all of a grid at one time.
Incorporate essay or role-play questions	Eliminate the need for ring-in by alternating between the teams so that teams have ample opportunity to answer without the pressure of ringing in. A team captain chooses the category and points. If the question is answered incorrectly, it can go to the next team in line or be offered to other teams.
	Increase the number of bonus questions and provide an extended period of time to answer the question.
Make a more strategy-based game	Insert numerous bonus questions that let teams wager their points throughout the game.
	Allow teams to wager on each question.
Add variety to the game	Arrange questions by activity type instead of by subject (for example, role play, physical activity).
Discourage teams from ringing in without knowing the answer (and randomly guessing)	Penalize incorrect answers (by the point value of the question, or even double the point value).
	Decrease the number of multiple-choice questions in your game.
	Shorten the answer timer so that teams have to respond to a question right away.

Family Feud Variations

If you want to . . .	Then . . .
Shorten game play	Drastically shorten the answer timer so that each contestant only has three to five seconds to answer. (This works best with fact-based information that requires quick recall.)
	Give teams one minute to brainstorm and record their answers; then quickly run through the questions with their prepared answers.
Have your answers indicate ranks or percentages, or be associated with values	Change the points awarded for uncovering each answer to be based on the rank, value, or percentage associated with that answer.
Emphasize a sequence or chronological process	Require that answers are uncovered in the proper order—from top to bottom or bottom to top. Don't count answers that are out of sequence as correct.
Have a procedure or a question that has many steps (or answers)	Break your question into several parts. For instance: "Name the first five steps you must do when performing CPR" could precede, "What are the final six steps in performing CPR?"
Use the game as a brainstorming session	Show the question to each team, and allow several minutes to brainstorm, record, and rank possible answers. The team in control of the board reads through their list, and if they can uncover every answer before getting three strikes, they win. If the opposing team gets a chance to steal, they choose one answer from their list that they feel has the highest potential.

If you want to . . .	Then . . .
Use the game as a brainstorming session (*continued*)	After the round, ask the teams to share some of their other answers or discuss the answers that were not uncovered.
Use the game as a quick energizer or an introduction or work with larger groups	Divide the room into two teams. Ask the first team to raise their hands and call out an answer. Alternate teams. Skip dividing the teams and have the trainees raise their hands and call out an answer. Hand out a small token prize for correct answers.

Tic-Tac-Dough Variations

If you want to . . .	Then . . .
Cover more content or have a longer, more complex game	Require a correct answer for a team to win a square (in other words, if the X team misses, the O team doesn't automatically win the square). Put several questions "behind" each square. To win that square, the team must answer all or a large portion of the questions correctly. Use a larger grid with contestants having to get four or five squares in a row to win.
Keep both teams engaged at all points during the game	Give the opposing team a chance to take the square if the first team gets the answer wrong. The team will get a limited time to call out the answer after the first team's answer is judged to be incorrect. After a team selects a square, allow either team to ring in to answer. Allow a short time for the team ringing in to answer the question (three seconds or less), or you'll have teams rushing to ring in and then trying to figure out the answer.

If you want to . . .	Then . . .
Emphasize strategy	Allow the option of "giving away" the question to the other team. In other words, if the X team gets a question that they think the other team can't answer, they can pass—forcing the O team to answer. If the O team is unable to answer, the X team gets the square.
Have multiple answers to a single question	Ask the same question for multiple squares, and reward a team when they get one of the many possible answers correct. Make note of what answers have already been given so teams don't repeat.
Encourage brainstorming or use role playing	Eliminate the ring-in timer, and allow the teams to collaborate on the answers or brainstorming topic for a specified amount of time. Have the teams take turns revealing their answers. The team with the best or closest answer gets the square.
Increase the number of people who can play the game	Break the two teams into smaller groups, and alternate between the individual groups on the two larger teams.
	Individual members on the larger team can take turns answering questions in a panel. Change the panel after a given amount of time.
Play in a *Hollywood Squares* game style	You may play *Tic-Tac-Dough* in a *Hollywood Squares* format using either video (prerecorded) experts or live experts. Experts are assigned to individual squares, or you may assign them to a designated row, just the "odd" or "even" squares, or portions of the board. You may have anywhere from one expert for each square to one expert for the entire game. When a trainee picks an expert's square, the question is revealed and asked to the expert.

If you want to . . .	Then . . .
Play in a *Hollywood Squares* game style (*continued*)	The expert gives a correct or an incorrect answer. The trainee has to decide whether he or she agrees or disagrees with the expert's given answer. If the trainee agrees or disagrees correctly, he or she gets the square. This format is great for larger groups and is very entertaining for an audience.
	You may also play a *Hollywood Squares* type of game without the use of an expert. Simply read a read a true-false question, and have trainees agree or disagree to win the space they've selected on the board. You can also have trainees explain why they agree or disagree for extra credit points.

Beat the Clock Variations

If you want to . . .	Then . . .
Speed up the game	Have all teams perform the same challenge at the same time and give points to the team that had the best results. (Here's where it will help to have an extra set of eyes.)
	Replace one of your matches with a speed round: hand out a written test and see how many questions they can answer in a designated period of time by dividing the pages of the test among the teammates. (You may also do this by seeing how many questions one team can answer orally in a given period of time.)

If you want to . . .	Then . . .
Add challenges	*Have teams:*
	Match up cards (that is, match products with benefits)
	Complete a speed round as described above
	Do brainstorming on easels
	Role-play scenarios and answers
	Build product or trade show displays
	Rank processes or procedures
	Answer a question; then perform a noncontent-related stunt for extra points
	Answer a question by popping balloons with the "wrong" answers on them, leaving only the balloon with the correct answer.
Use straightforward questions, but incorporate a simple level of physical stunts	*Have contestants:*
	Balance a simple object (like a ball) while answering a question
	Keep a balloon up in the air while answering a question
	Stand on one foot, or strike a balance-challenging pose while answering a question
	Write down their answers to a question on a piece of paper and try to get their paper to you before the other team
Incorporate more people	When there are large numbers of people on each team, have team captains choose which of their teammates will participate in a particular activity.

Wheel of Fortune Variations

If you want to . . .	Then . . .
Cover more content	Require the team to correctly answer a question prior to spinning the wheel. If they answer incorrectly, they lose the turn, the answer is displayed, and they forfeit spinning the wheel.
	Require the team to answer a final question before they can guess the word puzzle.
	Make the word puzzle at the end a final question that contestants must answer in order to win the game.
Reduce the element of chance due to the random spinning of the wheel	Keep the points on the wheel within a tight range (between 100 and 300 points) and eliminate the "Bankrupt" and "Lose a Turn" options.
	Award points only for answering a question correctly and give token prizes for wheel spins. This way, the game is dependent not on spinning the wheel but on answering questions correctly.
	On the wheel: instead of point values, have the categories of your questions or a number indicating the difficulty of a question. The "chance" then lies in the contestant's getting a particularly difficult or easy question or a category that he or she is more or less familiar with.
	Note: These variations reduce the reward or penalty for landing on certain sections of a wheel. There is still an element of chance in *Wheel of Fortune* no matter what modifications you make to the wheel.

If you want to . . .	Then . . .
Increase interactive training opportunities	Allow players or teams to act out or draw their answers without speaking.
	In addition to "Bankrupt," or "Free Turn" items on the wheel, include categories like "perform a skit" or "physical challenges."
Make the game more challenging	Use short or unique words for the word puzzle; there's more chance of guessing an incorrect letter.
Adjust the length of a game	Vary the word puzzle from a short, well-known word to a longer, less-known phrase (or essay).

Concentration Variations

If you want to . . .	Then . . .
Increase recognition of material	Require that contestants answer a question before selecting their panels (which could contain small prizes, objects, or pictures instead of questions and answers).
Vary the game play, or encourage collaboration	Rather than alternate between teams matching up pairs, give one team a minute to make as many matches as possible. Let the other team compete for the same length of time on another board. The team with more matches wins the round.
Decrease the length of a match	Use a smaller grid with fewer matching pieces.
	Reveal all the answers; then cover them up again and have contestants proceed to make matches.

If you want to . . .	Then . . .
Decrease the length of a match (continued)	Uncover all the questions, and have contestants just look for the matching answer.
	Number all the questions with even numbers and all the answers with odd numbers (or vice versa), and let contestants know which numbers designate answers or questions.
Remove the element of chance or memory in the game	Uncover all the questions and answers, and have contestants match pairs.
	Put a rebus behind the squares so that the contestants must solve the final puzzle in order to win the game.
Use more multimedia	Put pictures or play video in place of the question squares, have your trainees match the pictures or video with the answer squares.
	Use a video or graphic behind the squares to reveal a clue to a riddle or just have trainees identify what the picture or video is.
Vary game play and increase strategy	Have one team select a square and designate that the other team must try to select the matching square
	Have teams match identical question pairs, and give the answer to that question orally once they get a matching pair.

Who Wants to Be a Millionaire? Variations

If you want to . . .	Then . . .
Play in a shorter period of time	Have fewer "rungs" on the question ladder (perhaps five steps to get to the top instead of fifteen).
	Designate a period of time to answer, or shorten the length of the answer timer.
Have more than one contestant or team playing	Give a team the opportunity to climb the ladder until they miss a question; then go to the other team.
	Alternate between two teams, and turn the game into a race to reach the top of the ladder. If a team answers a question incorrectly, they stay at their present spot until they answer a question correctly.
Vary game play, or give each team more chances to get a question correct	You may add more lifelines during a match, such as:
	Mulligan: This allows the team to choose not to answer the question and answer an alternate question without losing a turn.
	Give away: This option allows one team to force the other team to try answering their question. This is particularly effective for keeping both teams on their toes at all times.
	Resource: This option allows the team to have a limited amount of time to consult any resource in the room. This could include their manual, the Internet, or other books.
Increase the difficulty level	Make some questions open-ended, essay, or role-play as trainees move up the ladder.

If you want to . . .	Then . . .
Incorporate brainstorming in your game	Open up a question to both teams. Whoever has the more appropriate answer moves up a rung on the ladder.
	Instead of multiple-choice questions, use open-ended questions to brainstorm. If a team comes up with the required number of reasonable answers, whether absolutely correct or not, they advance to the next rung.
Increase the level of competition	You can have both teams try to ring in to answer questions instead of alternating between teams.

College Bowl Variations

If you want to . . .	Then . . .
Shorten the game play	Reduce the bonus questions to only one per toss-up.
	Give teams an opportunity to pass on their bonus questions or forfeit the bonus without penalty.
	Eliminate the bonus questions after the toss-up.
Keep scores more balanced	Allow any team to answer bonus questions, not just the team that answered the preceding toss-up question.
	Reduce the value of the bonus questions and increase the value of the toss-up questions.
Make the game more strategic	Give the toss-up winner a chance to take the bonus questions for themselves, or pass them off to the other team.
	Have a penalty for answering bonus questions incorrectly.

If you want to . . .	Then . . .
Increase the challenge within the game	Vary the number of bonus questions based on question difficulty.
Make the game show more hands-on	Make the bonus questions role-play opportunities or brainstorming activities for both teams.

———

As we have seen, the ways in which you can change a TV game show are limited only by imagination. There are almost infinite ways to modify a game show's major elements to make it suit your training situation. In the next chapter, we explore modifying and setting up some of the elements that surround a game show to make it even more effective for your trainees.

Chapter 8

Teams, Titles, and Trinkets

In This Chapter, You Will:

- See how to designate and modify teams and judges.
- Read tips on setting up additional parameters like prizes, names, and titles.

The Title

The first thing that your trainees are going to see when they start a game show is the title of the game. You can name your game show anything you like as long as it is relevant to your students. It's not uncommon to use the type of game show in the title combined with the subject you're focusing on or the company name—for example:

- Safety Jeopardy!

- GreenWood Builder Squares

- Who Wants to Be a Call Center Pro?

You can also add "bowl" or "challenge" to any subject—for instance, the HIPPA Bowl or the Product Benefits Challenge. Be warned: the title that you choose will become known throughout your organization, so choose wisely.

Contestants and Teams

Things to consider:

- How are teams divided?

- Which team goes first, and how is this decided?

- Does the team need to have a captain?

- When and how should you assign a team captain?

- What are the captain's responsibilities?

- Is the captain or leader aware of the rules and his or her role?

- Can anyone on the team answer, or only a team captain?

On most television game shows, teams are set up so that an individual contestant is facing off against another single contestant. Each person wins or loses based on his or her intelligence, strategies, and strengths as a competitor. In the training environment, a more collaborative approach to competition is needed. This can be accomplished by dividing the trainees into teams. Entire teams can compete against each other, or select contestants can represent the whole team. Keep in mind that on a team, there can be both audience members and active contestants. Not everyone on a team needs to be directly involved with answering questions. There are several reasons for using teams:

> *Teams divide responsibility.* A team acting as a single contestant means that the wallflowers (those that wish to remain in the background) in the group can still help with the answers, but can hand over the job of answering the question to a more outgoing member of the team or a team leader. While some people want significance and recognition, reveling in the spotlight and showing off their brilliance, others feel very uncomfortable at the prospect of perceived public humiliation.
>
> *You are able to ask more in-depth questions* that require teams to discuss possible answers or formulate solutions. Learning improves when collaboration is involved.
>
> *Teams involve a greater number of people.* No one is left out or bored.
>
> *Each team has a better chance of answering any given question correctly.* You know the old (modified) adage: three to five heads are better than one.
>
> *Teams keep everyone engaged.* If certain members are answering a question, the other members can be cheering them on.

Teams provide some positive peer pressure. For example, if you want to assign reading for the next day's training session, you can mention that there will be a game show the next morning based on the reading. Individual trainees might brush this off and not do the reading—setting the whole class back. However, if they are responsible for contributing answers to a team, they won't want to let their team down or be the only person who didn't do their reading.

Here are a few things to keep in mind when having teams instead of contestants:

- If they're ringing in with a paddle, slammer, or other ring-in device, make sure that it is centrally located so that all team members have clear access.

- Consider selecting team leaders to represent their teams when answering a question. Their role will be important since they'll have to determine which answer to choose in the case of differing opinions within the group.

How you divide the teams is up to you and is typically based on the makeup of your class. If the class has a cross-section of different divisions or geographical territories, each grouping could be a team. However, it's no sin to break trainees out of predefined groups. This can work well to remove clique-type behavior within a group—one person always dominating, three "sucking up" to the dominating one, one who goes against anything the other four say, and another who is indifferent to the whole process of decision making within the group.

You can divide the teams by job functions (marketing versus sales, for example). You may also create multidisciplinary teams by scattering trainees with different job functions among several teams. Often the easiest and safest way to create teams is to divide trainees by where they are seated in the room (everyone on the left side is on team A, and everyone on the right side is on team B). If students are seated at several round tables, each of the tables becomes a team. We say that this is the "safest" way because it depersonalizes winning or losing. It is a lot less inflammatory if the right side beats the left side than if the marketing team smokes the sales department. Basically, you can divide the teams however you like, but we do recommend picking the teams yourself. Self-selected teams tend to be unbalanced, and the process of selection can be chaotic.

If your teams are large and time permits, rotate trainees in and out of rounds or matches to involve more people. Let's say that in a *Tic-Tac-Dough* game, you've divided the audience into two teams: the X team and the O team. During the first match, three people from each team answer the questions. During the second round, switch the three participants with three different people from the same team.

We recommend that you handpick the teams to give each team a good cross-section of experience and skill. For example, a seasoned pro combined with a new employee will yield better results than a team of new employees competing against a team of pros. Be wary, however, of selecting which members of a team will go up to answer a question if you are rotating contestants in and out of the game. A very competitive group may blame you for selecting the weaker members of their team if they lose.

Types of Contestants

In any given training class, there are five types of game show contestants:

The Competitor. The Competitors want to win at all costs. They need to have prominent significance and may be most useful when used as the spokesperson for the group. They may seem as if they are cocky or have something to prove and may become defensive if they are a lone contestant and get an answer wrong. These are the people who will argue with your judgment or will demand that you explain why they are wrong.

The King of Recall. They may not necessarily be smarter than anyone else, but they have the amazing ability to access information faster than anyone else. These will be the trainees who appear to be a sort of "idiot-savant." While they answer first (sometimes blurting out the answers), they aren't necessarily as good at explaining their answer or performing in a creative task.

The Wallflower. Wallflowers are like a deer in the headlights: they may very well know the answer to everything, but when they are put on the spot, they freeze. Forcing a contestant like this to be in the spotlight may make him or her very nervous or stressed. However, Wallflowers can be great team collaborators outside the spotlight.

The Collaborator. Collaborators could also be called Cheerleaders or the Peacemakers. They work well on the team and seek team consensus. Even if they don't always know the answers to everything, they are good at organizing the team to get the answers the team needs. They seek approval and feedback from everyone in a group. They are also great supporters, though they may not be interested in answering questions themselves.

The Reluctant Contestant. Some people just do not want to be on a team. Period. The fear of looking bad will prevent them from answering or participating. Reluctant Contestants may make better audience members than contestants—at least at first. They may be rotated into a team later if they seem to be getting into the game (and they usually do).

A team full of Competitors would be a nightmare, especially if they were pitted against the Wallflowers. A team of Collaborators would get along great but wouldn't get anywhere in a game show.

However, if these five contestant types are divided among the team, you have a spokesperson, a contributor, a cheerleader, the information person, and the collaborator who makes sure everyone has a chance to contribute.

Number of Teams

Over the years we have seen game shows played with as many as ten teams competing in a *Jeopardy!* or *College Bowl* game. However, more than five teams can become unwieldy and hard to control. With more teams, game shows take more time, and the participants have a reduced opportunity to answer questions and participate. In the case of the trainer with ten teams, her rationale was that the salespeople had come from ten regions across the country, and each region should have its own team. Although we understand what she was thinking, a better solution would have been to combine regions to make four or five teams.

Team Leaders

A team leader can be your most valuable asset in a game show. Team leaders can be:

> *The Mouthpiece:* The team leader can be the one to give the answers. You'll know exactly who to call on when a team answers, and you'll get only one answer from each team, not a bunch of shouted indiscernible answers.

> *The Facilitator:* The team leader can guide discussions. You don't have to be the one to get the teams back on track in a discussion or try to spur on the brainstorming.

> *The Negotiator:* The team leader can collaborate with the group to arrive at one final answer.

> *The Babysitter:* The team leader controls rowdy behavior within the group. You don't have to worry about calming everyone down when they get overly enthusiastic.

The Cheerleader: Humans learn best when they're in a safe environment. The team leader can make sure that all players are supported, listened to, and encouraged so that your trainees walk away with the most information.

The team leader can have any combination of these responsibilities, but a leader who is the facilitator or babysitter may want to designate another "mouthpiece of the team" in order to avoid dominating team play.

Select team leaders before you even mention the game show. If you already know them, you may want to bring them into the training session ten minutes early so you can explain their roles to them. If you don't already know your trainees, take a short break before you play the first match to pick and explain the role to the people you chose to be leaders. You may also decide to switch team leaders every game or match to vary responsibility, or who gets to "give" the answers.

If you don't have time to get to know the trainees, you may let the teams pick their own leader. This can be done by team consensus or by designating the first person to stand up. If you're concerned that the teams may select the most domineering person, ask the team leaders to stand up at the end of the selection process. At this point say, "Okay, great. The person to your right will be the team leader."

There are several types of people who can be a team leader:

The Random Leader: The team picks a leader at random, typically the most vocal member of a team. This team leader should be a Mouthpiece or a Negotiator.

The Wallflower: Involve the Wallflower of a team by making this person a team leader without the responsibility of being the Mouthpiece.

Upper Management: If you have a group like a region and the regional leaders are also in your training, you may designate the regional leader to be a team leader. Nevertheless, still consider breaking teams up cross-regionally.

The Rowdy Player: Players who are consistently acting up tend to settle down if given the responsibility of keeping the whole team under control. Have this player designate an alternate Mouthpiece for the team.

When briefing team leaders, you don't need to go into the intricacies of being a leader; you simply need to say that they set the example for their team's behavior and should ultimately be supportive of all their members. You should also give them a clear explanation of their basic responsibilities, like answering for the team or encouraging collaboration.

Table 8.1 explains the roles that a particular type of leader will typically (or is most comfortable to) fulfill.

Team Names

Another consideration in the game show is naming the teams. At some point you will need to refer to the teams by a name, even if you call them by number or region. You always have the option to let the teams decide their own names—in which case the results can be somewhat humorous but unpredictable. Heaven forbid that in this PC society anyone would think to call themselves something racy, political, or otherwise offensive, but it could happen. Most people generally stick to tame team names, and this kind of team-building activity can break the ice among teammates. We recommend reserving the right to veto names before telling trainees to start making up their own names. When you pick the team names yourself, you eliminate the possibility of the teams' choosing something offensive, and you have the added benefit of being able to name the teams after important content or key words. But in the process, you lose the team-building and introduction opportunity.

Table 8.1. Leadership Types and Roles

	The Mouthpiece	The Facilitator	The Negotiator	The Babysitter	The Cheerleader
The Random Leader	X		X	X	X
The Wallflower		X	X		X
Upper Management		X			X
The Rowdy Player			X	X	X

Judging

Here are some things for you or your judge to consider overall:

- How are questions answered? For instance, do they have to be answered in the form of a question?

- Is everyone required to participate in a role-play scenario or only part of the team?

- Who judges whether the answers are correct: you or the judge?

- If a given answer is unclear, do contestants have the opportunity to clarify before it is judged? For example, suppose the correct answer is "vice president and president" and the contestant answers "executive group." Can you ask for more information, or is the answer considered wrong?

- If an answer is correct:

    Are points awarded, and if so, how many?
    What happens next? Who gets control of the board?

- If an answer is incorrect:

    Are points deducted?
    Does the team lose control of the board?
    Can teams get partial credit for an answer?

- How are disputes handled?

    Can points awarded be reversed?
    Is there a "statute of limitations" on awarding or deducting points?
    Are judges' decisions final?

Judgment Calls

There are bound to be different times throughout the course of the game show where you will need to have some kind of judgment call:

- *Determining whether a player or team answer is correct.*
- *Handling "shades of gray" issues.* Let's say that during a *Family Feud* game, the correct answer is "evergreen" and a contestant answers "pine tree." The answer is in the same category but is not an exact match with the answer hidden on the board. The judge has the authority to determine whether the answer is close enough.
- *Moderating answer disputes.* If the answer is technically incorrect but the team can defend the answer, it can be worthwhile to listen to their objections. A change in ruling may be in order. Conversely, in the interest of winning, opposing teams may object to the correctness of another team's answer and may wish to argue their case.
- *Discerning who rang in first.* If you are using ring-in devices that are not electronic (like bells, whistles, chimes, animal sounds, or hand raising), it can be difficult to determine who was the first to ring in while reading the question. You can help the judges in this area by assigning either distinctive auditory ring-in devices (each team has a different, distinct-sounding instrument or call) or by requiring teams to give a visual ring-in cue (such as raising their hands or putting up colored flags).
- *Determining whether a contestant has answered before the answer time elapses.*
- *Handling basic rule infractions.* For instance, if you have a rule that only the team captain is supposed to answer, but another team member blurts out the answer, the judge observes and handles this rule infringement.

Advantages of a Judge

Of course, the host can make judgment calls, but there are many advantages to using a separate judge:

- Judges keep you off the hot spot. Determining right and wrong answers can be controversial, and having a separate judge can keep you out of the fray.

- Judges can be content experts, with the ability to elaborate and add instructive commentary with their decisions.

- Judges are a support system that helps you to focus on your job of instruction and hosting.

- When you have a judge, you don't have to remember all the answers. If you're uncertain whether an answer is correct, the judge with the answer key can give you a thumbs up or thumbs down.

- Judges can sully their hands with score deductions for rowdy or unsportsmanlike behaviors. The more impartial you are, the better. You can be the good guy interested in training instead of having to be the disciplinarian.

While judges can make your job a lot easier, we don't want to scare you here. Usually one person can serve as a host, trainer, and judge without difficulty. If you're doing a quick game to preview or serve as an icebreaker or an energizer, a judge probably isn't necessary. If you are doing a large production-style game show or a game that lasts thirty minutes or more, judges are often a necessity. In a game show where stakes and competition are high, having separate judges is even more important.

Who Should Judge?

Trainees in your class. If you have a trainee who knows your content better than any of the other trainees, one way to even out this disparity is to let that student be a judge instead of a team player. Conversely, if you have a trainee who knows the material less than any of the other trainees or has missed some of the training, give this person an answer key and ask him or her to help you.

Content experts. Let's say you're training your staff on the ins and outs of a new drug that your company manufactures. Inviting in one of the lead developers will give this person an opportunity to interact with the trainees. This person can add information that only he or she would know, and trainees will have an opportunity to ask questions.

Department heads and supervisors. There's nothing better than having the opportunity to make yourself look good in front of your staff. Providing supervisors with the opportunity to be a "guest expert" or judge will give them time with the trainees. Your trainees may appreciate being able to show off their knowledge in front of their supervisors, and you may appreciate the opportunity to show off your game show hosting in front of your supervisors.

Administrative staff. Getting the administrative staff in front of your trainees will allow them to get to know them (if they don't already) and put them into the spotlight.

Something to keep in mind: you can serve as the judge and bring in a colleague or even a student to be the host of the game. Make sure they understand the rules and the answers, and have been properly briefed on the art of hosting. (We suggest having them read Chapter Thirteen.)

Using the Judge

Judges can be your biggest allies when hosting a game show. To ensure that the judging experience goes smoothly for both you and your selected judge, there are a few guidelines to follow:

- Clearly define the judge's responsibilities ahead of time. You may want to share some of the judging responsibilities. For instance, if you are the content expert, you can determine the accuracy of the answers and leave other judging activities to the designated judge.
- Introduce the judge to the class and let him or her know specifically when judgment calls will be made.
- Respect the judge's decisions as final. If you have questions about the credibility of the judge, so will the contestants. Chaos will surely ensue.
- Make sure that the judges know the rules of play, as well as the questions and answers. It goes without saying that if judges are monitoring the rules, they should probably know what they're monitoring. To be sure they do, give them a copy of the rules and a copy of the answer key. Discuss with the judge the amount of discretion that you'd like to allow for answers and penalties.
- Work out ahead of time how you will be calling on judges for their answers or how they should signal you for rulings.
- Seat the judges where they can clearly see and hear the contestants and where you and the trainees can see and hear the judges.
- Feel free to use a panel of judges if the judging requires different disciplines. For instance, if you're playing a game show about a new product launch, bring in the new product manager to talk about the features and the sales manager to handle questions about the sales of the product.

Prizes

Prizes are a nice extra but not a necessary component in a training game show. If you would like to give away token prizes to winning teams or contestants, that's fine. However, most people generate the desire to win simply for the pride of winning. If you've ever played a board game with friends or family, you were playing because it would bring you prestige or bragging rights, not because you thought there was going to be a twenty-seven-inch plasma screen TV waiting outside. This same principle applies for your trainees. They may ask you what they're "going to get" if they win, but they'll play the game show simply for the sake of winning (or just for the sake of playing a game). Prizes are fun and cute and neat, and there's nothing wrong with giving away stickers or pencils or something else, but don't feel obligated to hand them out, and definitely don't go overboard.

If your game is set up so that only a select group of trainees is playing at a time (rather than the entire group or team), you can award prizes to them on an individual basis. You could then offer a second-level prize to the teammates who cheered them on. For instance, if there is a ten-member team and time for only four members to be contestants, they can play for their own prize as well as prizes for their entire team. If you're going to be awarding prizes, it's not a bad idea to give smaller prizes to the other (nonwinning) teams as well so everyone can walk away with a gift.

Part of the fun of prizes is the ceremonial act of awarding them. It fits in well with the tone of a game show and boosts the excitement even more as contestants cheer on their wins.

It's okay for prizes to be hokey and cheap. After all, it's not the prize that counts; it's the information in the game show. In addition, there is danger in giving away highly valued prizes: the games quickly become about winning the prize rather than learning the content. Big prizes can also increase trainer scrutiny; members of a team will be quick to pounce on you if they think you made a bad call, a mistake, or an error in judgment.

Case Study: The (Non)Importance of Prizes

We were hosting a game show at a national sales meeting. Our client wanted to offer a $100 gift certificate to each member of the winning team. We talked the client into putting her prize budget to better use and came up with an alternate prize: the hotel hygiene kit (complete with the little soap, shampoo, and moisturizers). We offered to have their prizes "delivered" to their rooms so that they would be there when they were done with the meeting. The fact that this worthless prize had been sitting in their hotel rooms all along was completely irrelevant to them. The teams really got into playing the game show. In fact, at one point we leveled with the contestants: "Look, you guys *do* realize that you're playing for a trial-sized shampoo bottle that is already in your rooms, don't you?" The teams remained as enthusiastic as they had been before. It truly didn't matter to them what they were getting: they just wanted to win.

The point was that although we were giving the contestants something completely worthless (and that we didn't have to pay for), they still valued winning the game show and were still excited, enthusiastic participants.

How you pick your prizes or whether you decide to use them at all is completely up to you. The best prizes are small and have something to do with the training at hand.

Tip: Ideas for Prizes

- Give each team member or contestant play money for each of the points he or she generates. The members can then exchange the points for prizes in an auction or "garage sale," or they can win the play money for pride's sake.

- Company T-shirts

- Cheap toys from the dollar store (stress balls or jacks, for example)

- Books that support your content

- Certificates of achievement (either computer printouts or official-looking certificates purchased from an office supply store)

- Company giveaways or left-over trade show "swag" like pencils, magnets, or stickers

- An extra-long lunch break or a paid day off

- Gift coupons in value of one to five dollars for coffee or fast food

- A chance to make their boss do something (wear a wig to work one day, get them coffee, call them "Sir Magnificent" for a day). Remember to ask before offering anyone's services.

To create the most effective training space, align every element of the game show to your training goals, from the prizes to the category names. For example, you could have the "Safety Feud" with toy builder figurines as prizes, the "Hazardous Hyenas" and the "OSHA Orcas" teams, and the team captains can be the "foreman." The game show will leave a strong overall safety impression with your trainees.

Now that we've seen a sampling of the ways to customize game shows in both rules and surrounding elements, you know that game shows can be made to fit most any training scenario and purpose and that customizing your game show is often both necessary and crucial. In the next section, we'll explore an equally critical part of the game show: writing the game show questions.

Part III

Writing Effective Questions

The chapters in Part Three eliminate the guesswork about writing good questions. A game show can go from exciting to tedious in a matter of seconds if the questions are confusing or confounding, or don't relate to the training. Our goal is to help you avoid that by giving you tried-and-true methods and tips for writing the best questions to fit your content and your training.

Chapter 9

Question Types and Tips

- Matching
- Multiple Answer
- Sequencing
- Open-Ended
- Essay/Role Play
- True-False

In This Chapter, You Will:

- Find explanations of different question formats and their purpose in your game show.
- See tips for creating different types of questions.

A lot of people initially think that it's the rules, board, glitz, and other components that make up an effective game show. Because of this, they often ignore the most important part of a game: the questions. Without good questions, you can't convey content properly, your trainees get confused, and game play is interrupted by the questions instead of being driven by them.

We're going to examine how to write effective game show questions in a variety of question formats:

- Multiple choice

- Matching

- Multiple answer

- Sequencing

- Open-ended

- Essay and role play

- True-false

For each of these formats, we'll give an explanation, set out the advantages and disadvantages of the questions, and provide tips for writing each type of question.

Multiple Choice

Multiple-choice questions are commonly found in training game shows. A question or statement—George Washington was the _____ president of the United States—is followed by multiple answer options—(a) First (b) Last (c) Sixteenth. On TV you'll notice that the only place you'll find a multiple-choice question is on *Who Wants to Be a Millionaire?* where contestants have time to consider their four answer options for a significant amount of time.

Multiple-choice questions take longer to read, and unless the contestant has the answer right away, he or she will need time to think through and eliminate the answers to determine which one is most appropriate. If you're going to use multiple-choice questions, consider lengthening the time you allow the contestants to read before having to ring in.

Strength

- Multiple-choice questions are easier to judge since the answers are provided, thereby restricting the amount of answer variation.

Limitation

- Multiple-choice questions are difficult to create compared to other types of questions and they accommodate random guesses.

 ## Tips for Writing Multiple-Choice Questions

- Questions may be written as either direct questions or incomplete statements. Direct questions are easier to read than incomplete statements:

  Less effective:

  The capital of Minnesota is _____.

  a. Minneapolis

  b. St. Paul

  c. Winona

  d. St. Cloud

  More effective:

  Which city is the capital of Minnesota?

  a. Minneapolis

  b. St. Paul

  c. Winona

  d. St. Cloud

- If you use an incomplete statement, place the blanks at the end of the question rather than in the beginning or middle of it.

- Include most information in the question rather than the answer options to make reading and responding to the question a more efficient process.

- Make sure that the incorrect answer options are as plausible as the correct answer to students who don't know the content. For instance, you shouldn't have a question like this: "What is the Swedish word for *nice?*" when the answer set looks like this:

  a. Bien

  b. *Trevlig*

  c. Merci

  d. Danke

  It's fairly obvious to anyone studying Swedish that only one of the words is in Swedish (the rest of the words are in Spanish, French, and German), so answer b is a good guess, even if you have no clue how to say "nice" in Swedish.

Matching

In matching questions of the simplest form, players identify two similar parts. Matching questions are mainly applicable to *Concentration* games but can also be used in a *Beat the Clock* game or any others where you incorporate longer challenges. These questions can be used in a variety of ways:

- Two halves of one concept can be presented. For example, if you were training in leadership practices, the opening phrase, "Followers shouldn't be expected to go anywhere . . ." could be matched up to the closing phrase ". . . that their leader is unwilling to lead."

- A question and answer could be a match. For example, "What does the golden rule say?" would match up with, "Treat others as you would like to be treated."

- Acronyms can be matched with their meanings. For example, if you were teaching company lingo, on one panel there might be the acronym A.S.L.; the matching panel could have the words that A.S.L. stands for: "American Sign Language."

- Several parts of a concept can be paired with one overarching theme (this is also called categorizing). For example, you could have the trainees match up the different parts of a form with their proper document, or you could have several species of animals, and the question involves matching them with their correct genus.

Strengths

- Matching questions can be used in three forms: matching up cards (physically matching a card with a picture or question on it with another card containing a picture or answer from a large group of cards), word-line matching (see the example in Tips for Writing Matching Questions), and *Concentration*-like card flip over (where questions and answers are hidden and the contestant has to flip over the correctly matching pair partially by memory and partially by random chance).

- The matching-question format is great for hands-on and interactive activities.

- These questions can help establish relationships between concepts.

Limitations

- Matching questions can rely heavily on memory alone.

- These questions can become complex and take time to answer.

- Matching questions encourage, or are more accommodating of, blind guessing.

 ## Tips for Writing Matching Questions

- Be sure to differentiate between concepts so that one part of a match couldn't correctly be paired with several others. For example, your question shouldn't look like this:

  Draw a line to match the people with their correct numbers:
  Number of Trainers in our organization   Six
  Number of Executives in our organization   Seven
  Number of Sales Managers in our organization   Less than ten

  This is an extreme example, but a question like this would become a nightmare. Even if there are different numbers of trainers, executives, and sales managers, the answer "less than ten" applies to all of them.

- Ask follow-up questions to avoid blind guessing. One of the disadvantages of matching questions like you see in *Concentration* is that a contestant can inadvertently uncover a match without knowing that the two halves are related to each other. Ask a very closely related (and relatively easy) follow-up question after the match is uncovered to ensure that the trainee is absorbing the information.

Multiple Answer

Multiple-answer questions look like multiple-choice questions with more than one correct answer. They can be difficult to answer rapidly because each answer takes time to process. These also tend to be tougher to just guess at since they can't be narrowed to just one choice. Because of the difficulty level, multiple-answer questions are not used frequently in a game show—with the exception of brainstorming activities and in *Family Feud*. A multiple-answer question looks like this:

Which two of the following four states border Minnesota?
a. Illinois
b. *Wisconsin*
c. Ohio
d. *Iowa*

You may also ask a form of true-false question with a multiple-answer format—for example:

Which of the following statements are true?
a. Leadership can be taught.
b. A leader is always a good boss.
c. Some people are naturally better leaders than others.
d. Every workplace needs some leaders.
e. Leaders are more fun than "normal" people.

Strength

- Multiple-answer questions are more challenging than multiple choice and make it almost impossible to employ the strategy of blind guessing.

Limitation

- These questions can be difficult to answer and are much more time-consuming than others for contestants to read, process, and then answer.

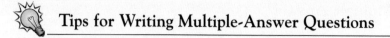

Tips for Writing Multiple-Answer Questions

- Attach a number to the question to clarify what you are looking for. For example, in the question about which states border Minnesota, the writer specified that the player name two states.

- If you are asking a question that has multiple, nonlist answers, specify how many answers you are looking for—for example:

  What is the process by which plants convert light into energy? (2 answers)
  a. *Photosynthesis*
  b. *Chlorophyll converts light into sugars*
  c. Light molecules produce energy reactions in the nucleus

- The same basic tips apply for writing multiple-answer questions as for writing multiple-choice questions. Make sure that all listed answers are as close to being plausible as the correct answers (or at least good distracters) and that most of the information is in the questions, not in the answers.

Sequencing

Sequencing questions are typically open-ended questions that have multiple steps following a distinct order. These questions are good for dealing with content based around processes and procedures since they require steps that must be performed in a certain order. For example, if you were training employees how to handle discipline issues you might pose the question:

Rank in order (from first to last) the following corrective actions that should be taken after you are informed of a sexual harassment incident:

_____ Give a verbal warning.

_____ Interview all parties.

_____ Contact human resources.

_____ Terminate the aggressor.

_____ Issue a written warning.

Strengths

- These allow players to practice working out processes and procedures.

- These questions allow players to visually sequence items and make good physical and interactive challenges.

Limitation

- Sequencing questions can get complex and take a longer period of time to answer than other questions.

Tips for Writing Sequencing Questions

- Be sure to specify in which direction you want contestants to list the sequence. For example, specify whether they should list developments from most current to least current or numbers from highest to lowest—or vice versa.

- Although sequencing questions can be useful for putting processes in order, sequencing too many elements can be tedious. What if a contestant gets almost all of the twelve-part sequence correct but reverses the order of the last two elements? Your trainee would be very frustrated because it took thought and concentration to sequence twelve elements, and they were *almost* all correct. To avoid this situation, consider:

> Breaking up long sequences into sequences with four or five elements. For example, you may have a question that lists the "first five procedures in developing a marketing handout" and another question that lists the "last five procedures in developing a marketing handout." Since the questions are not dependent on each other, they may appear at any point in the game.

> Giving partial credit for a sequence that is mostly correct, or scoring based on the number of elements that they have in the right place instead of on the correct sequence as a whole.

Open-Ended

Open-ended questions require trainees to spontaneously recall information, with no answer options provided. These questions also allow trainees the freedom to answer in several different ways, but they aren't as expansive as an essay or role-play question.

Strengths

- Open-ended questions are great for team collaboration and longer activities.

- These questions are appropriately difficult; no one can blind-guess an answer.

Limitations

- Open-ended questions can take considerable time to answer.

- By their very nature, open-ended questions induce a wide variety of answers—but not necessarily the specific answer that you're looking for.

Tips for Writing Open-Ended Questions

- Open-ended questions usually work best if they begin with a verb or a question word. Using a verb helps the contestant to know how he or she should answer the question. It's direct and to the point:

Verb	Example
Give: You provide the answer.	"Give the month, day, and year of D-Day in World War II."
Name: You identify the name, title, country, or other category.	"Name the vice president of marketing."
Define: You give the precise meaning.	"Define *synergy*."
Explain: You should make something clear or describe how to do something.	"Explain the three steps of a benefits-driven sale."
List: You should name multiple answers, in order or one after another.	"List the four steps to filling out a project change form." "List the presidents on Mount Rushmore."

- Use *question* words to help the contestant discern what type of information they need to give: *Who, What, Where, When, Why, or How:*

Question Word	Example
Who: Name the person or organization.	"Who wrote 'The Tell-Tale Heart'"?
What: Name the action or fact.	"What should you do if there is a C9–4 emergency?"

Question Word	Example
Where: Give the location.	"Where is our corporate headquarters?"
When: Give the time.	"When is the best time to ask for a raise (within a month)?"
Why: Give the reason, or explain.	"Why should a person always submit the F-4 personnel form before the Z-59 form? Give three reasons."
How: Describe or explain an action or process.	"How should you end every transaction with a customer?"

- The two forms (verb first or question word first) are interchangeable. One fits into a question form, and the other is a request or command. For example you might ask, "Who is the new vice president of sales?" or "Name the new vice president of sales." Either a verb or a question word will work. Use whichever form you're comfortable with and sounds most clear.

- With short-answer questions that require a numerical response, specify the degree of precision that is expected at the start of the question—for example: "Within $500, what is the base price of a Toyota Corolla?" If the price is $16,000, any answer between $15,500 and $16,500 would be accepted.

Essay and Role Play

Essay and role-play questions are open-ended questions with more detailed answers or that involve completing a given task. For example, you may want to ask trainees to role-play being a call center operator dealing with an angry customer. You may want them to discuss an at-work scenario in depth. This is where inserting a role-play or essay question into your game show can be useful.

Strengths

- Generally essay and role-play questions engage students well, offering a change of pace in the game or drawing out critical thinking.

- Essay and role-play questions work well for team collaboration and can be used to introduce and acclimate teams to each other.

Limitations

- Essay and role-play questions can take a long time to explain and complete.

- These are difficult to judge; whether a scenario was correctly played is subjective.

Tips for Writing Essay and Role-Play Questions

- If you have a particularly long or complex scenario, keep the scenario and the question up on the computer screen, projector, or whiteboard during discussion so that contestants can refer to the material while developing their answer.

- You can use handouts on a long or complex scenario. If the trainees are all working on the same question, they can take the handout and use another room or space to formulate their answers.

- As with open-ended questions, be specific about what you're looking for. If you present the scenario, "Act out a good leadership exchange," you may want players to present an exchange portraying their current work experiences or executive leaders, but the responses that you get may range from acting out a soccer coaching scene to a parent-child interaction.

- You may want to give key points or steps that trainees should touch on in their presentation, for example, "Act out a good leadership exchange that includes the three steps of positive leadership."

True-False

True-false questions are just that: true or false. A statement is proposed (True or false: Lincoln was the first U.S. president) and the contestant answers one way or another (Answer: False). These questions are not regularly used in game shows and for obvious reasons should not be used in types of game shows that allow a team to answer a question that another team has answered incorrectly.

Strengths

- True-false questions can be answered quickly, change the pace of a game, and require critical thinking skills.

- These are often good to springboard discussion. For example, they can be used to dispel popular myths. If the whole class thinks that an answer is false and it is really true, the trainer can explain both why the trainees might think the question is false and why it is true.

Limitations

- True-false questions allow trainees to have a high percentage of correct answers while blindly guessing (fifty-fifty, in fact!).

- These questions don't allow the trainees to expound on what they know unless you add a "justify your answer" element, where trainees have to explain why they answered true or false.

- It is tough to control the difficulty level of a true-false question. They have the tendency to be either too easy or too tricky or difficult.

Tips for Writing True-False Questions

- While true-false questions may seem to be the easiest of all questions to write, they can become the most complicated overall. The statement that is given has to be completely true or completely false. An ambiguous statement can lead to arguments. Consider the question, "True or false: The sky is blue." While the obvious answer would be "true," it can be argued that the sky is not blue at night. Even if you qualify the statement by saying, "True or false: The sky is blue during the day," it can be argued that the statement could be false on days that are overcast or stormy. It is a basic fact of competitive game shows that if an answer can be argued, it will be argued. If you want to use true-false questions, make sure that they are as clear as possible.

- In any question, avoid making a correct answer one of opinion instead of fact. With true-false questions, be particularly careful. For example, if you wrote: "True or false: Global warming is occurring," some people would argue that there are many scientific theories on global warming and thus they could not state with the certainty of true or false that the statement was incorrect or correct. Instead you could write: "True or false:

According to some environmentalists, global warming is occurring" or "True or false: Some evidence supports the scenario that global warming is occurring." These are good questions to have follow-up discussions about or to elaborate on after the answer has been revealed.

Now that you've seen the types of questions that you can use in a game show and some question-specific tips, the next chapter explores general rules for writing any type of question.

Chapter 10

Effective Question Writing

In This Chapter, You Will:

- Learn the most effective ways to write a question for your game show.
- Use a checklist to make sure you're on the right track with your questions.

The way that you phrase or write a question can have a surprising impact on the effectiveness of your game. Effective question writing is particularly important in games that require ring-in. If a question isn't clear, it can stop the whole game or inspire trainees to comment on the fairness of the game. You've seen tips on writing individual types of questions; however, there are certain rules that can be applied to all types of questions.

Make Sure the Questions Are Relevant

Unless you are doing an icebreaker, the questions should relate to the topic that you are training. If the game show is not relevant, the information in the game becomes harder for your participants to digest. They will also see the game show as just a game and not a learning tool. Some participants may resent their time being wasted on a game that has no perceived connection to the training session.

Be Clear

You would prefer to have the audience think about answering the question rather than trying to decipher what the question means. Consider the following two questions that have the same content:

What is the current interest rate of a twenty-year fixed-rate mortgage?
Clear and to the point. When in doubt, keep it simple.

If a consumer selects a twenty-year mortgage, what interest rate could he expect to pay if he has negotiated the mortgage today?
Not so clear. Trainees may have to read it two or three times to understand exactly what it is asking.

Be Specific

With any team's answer, you look for a certain degree of precision and accuracy. In order to prompt the answers you are seeking, the question in the game show has to be specific and accurate:

- Clear up confusion by specifying exactly what you are looking for in the subject of your question. For example, instead of asking, "Who was the first president?" ask, "Who was the first president of the United States?"

- Whenever you are asking for numbers and you don't require an *exact* answer, specify the range that you are looking for. For example, instead of asking, "What is the cost of a Toyota Corolla?" ask, "Within $500, what is the base price of a Toyota Corolla SE?"

- If you're asking about multiple events or an event or subject that has occurred more than once, specify which event you are referring to. For example, instead of asking, "Name one of the hurricanes that hit Florida this year," ask, "Name the *first* hurricane that hit Florida in 2005."

Be Direct

This tip is closely related to being clear. When you're asking a question, be succinct:

- Get to the point. The faster you get to what you want to ask in a question, the smoother the game play will go. Instead of asking, "You think a colleague is having a heart attack. What are the three most common signs to determine if this is actually the case?" ask, "Name the three most common symptoms of a heart attack."

- Don't use your answers to convey information that the question needs to ask. Although you should strive to be direct, you shouldn't leave out so much information that it has to be revealed in the answers. For example, instead of asking a question like this:

John Smith is:
a. the vice president of operations for the eastern branch.
b. the vice president of operations for the western branch.
c. the vice president of operations for the southern branch.

ask:

John Smith is the vice president of operations for which branch?
a. Eastern
b. Western
c. Southern

Have Only One Correct Answer

You may know exactly what answer you're looking for, but if the question is unclear or could be interpreted in a different way, could someone come up with another answer? Could someone who is thinking creatively come up with a different, but valid and correct, response?

A question with multiple answers, as we have seen, is, "What color is the sky?" The answer of "blue" seems clear, but the sky could be gray on any given day. It could be considered black at the nighttime or red in the morning and evening hours. This seems to be a relatively elementary question, but you can see how being ambiguous in question writing can inspire a creative wealth of answers. Instead, ask: "The sky is _____ during the day because it reflects all colors but this one."

Although having discrepancies in the correct answers is good for generating discussion, it's a mini-nightmare when it comes to running a game show smoothly. If you *do* want there to be more than one correct answer, try using open-ended questions to generate brainstorming, or use *Family Feud* to accommodate multiple answers.

Another example of having multiple answers is with homographs: words that are spelled the same but have different meanings. A situation in training where this would cause confusion is rare but can happen. For example, instead of asking, "Where would you find a bank in Minneapolis?" ask, "Where in Minneapolis's natural landscape would you find a river bank?" In this way, the players wouldn't name where you could find the closest ATM but rather where you would find a river bank.

Don't Give Anything Away

One game show question shouldn't give clues to another question or be based on the response of another question for a couple of reasons:

- If you're playing a game show where contestants can freely select their own questions, inevitably there will be a question that doesn't make sense.

- Since a game is very competitive, if a team gets a question where a clue had been given earlier in the game, it will be seen as an unfair advantage.

For example, if you are writing a question about leadership, neither one of your questions should say, "This is the other half of being a good leader." Automatically it raises the question, "What was the first half?"

When writing any type of question, always check to be sure that your question doesn't give away your answer. For example, if you had the question, "Spell *lasagna*," it wouldn't be difficult to answer that question. A good alternative would be to write: "Spell _____" Then read the word *lasagna*, show a picture, or write the phonetic pronunciation from a dictionary.

Avoid Complex Sentences

There are certainly scenarios that call for complex sentences because they contain complex situations like some role-playing and essay questions. In these cases, participants are allowed more time to answer and think about a question (and reread it if necessary). However, a simple short-answer question in *Jeopardy!* should never contain a question like this:

> Billy gets on a train going from Orlando to Minneapolis; the train now contains forty-two people. On the way, two passengers get off in Little Rock and four more get on. If thirteen get off in St. Louis and half the sum of the original passengers plus the number of passengers that got on in Little Rock get on, what is the name of the city Billy is going to?

This is a bit of an exaggerated example, but you get the point: keep the questions simple whenever possible.

Be Accurate

Always check your questions and answers for accuracy before playing the game. Everyone makes mistakes, but when the competition level is high, a simple mistake can cause quite a ruckus.

- Check your facts. Of course you know the material inside out, but make sure that a simple typing error doesn't make your facts fiction. For example, if you asked, "Name the five presidents on Mount Rushmore," not only would your contestants be confused (because there are only four presidents on Mount Rushmore), but they may be upset if their answer of the four presidents was counted incorrect (or if their fictional fifth president is discounted).

- Make sure the basics are correct. Punctuation, spelling, and grammar are all important to check before you play the game show with your trainees. Some software programs have spell and grammar checkers built in and if you're typing up your questions, most word processing programs have these features as well. However, although these checkers are helpful, they shouldn't replace good proofreading.

Effective Questions Checklist

____ Is the item an appropriate assessment of the content or learning objective?

____ Is the question direct, specific, and accurate?

____ Is only one answer clearly correct (in non-*Feud* games, or non-multianswer questions)?

____ Is the question clearly worded and stated in language appropriate for your trainees?

____ Can the item be answered briefly and concisely using a single word or short phrase (in non-role-play and essay questions)?

____ Is everything in the question correct: facts, spelling, and language?

____ If questions are multiple choice:

Is the majority of the content located in the question (not the answer choices)?

Are all response options equivalent in length, style, format, and grammar?

Are all incorrect answer options as plausible as the correct answer?

Need to Know vs. Nice to Know: Deciding Whether a Question Stays or Goes

- Does the question revolve around your content?

- If you're doing a review, did you cover the question material in class?

- Is the question going to further your trainees' understanding of the subject matter?

- Is the material crucial to the trainees' success on a test or in the workplace?

- Are you able to cover the appropriate depth with the question?

These basic rules and the previous chapter's individual question tips will help you write questions that will be successful in your game show (and allow you to have the successful game show). However, not all questions work well within a game show, depending on what you wish to accomplish. The next chapter explores choosing question types based on your training content and purpose.

Chapter 11

Questions to Fit Your Purpose

In This Chapter, You Will:

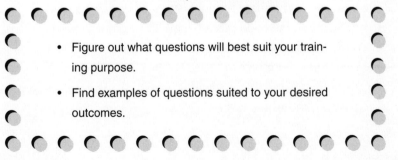

- Figure out what questions will best suit your training purpose.
- Find examples of questions suited to your desired outcomes.

This chapter will help guide you through developing questions depending on your needs. We'll examine questions designed to:

- Preview a topic

- Review a topic

- Generate brainstorming

- Energize a training session

- Work as icebreakers

- Conduct a role-playing exercise

Questions to Preview a Topic

When you're writing questions for a game show that is going to preview material, the question should do one of the following:

- Stimulate thought and arouse curiosity

- Show why a topic is important and relevant

- See what trainees need to learn (gaps in their knowledge)

To Stimulate Thought and Arouse Curiosity

The best way to stimulate thought is to give students a roadway for their thought and not add speed bumps. Open-ended questions that let trainees reflect on their own experiences are effective to get them thinking about your subject. For instance, if you're conducting a training session on customer service for bank employees, you could ask questions like these:

"Name the top five complaints consumers have about banking."

"Name three ways you can interact with a customer to make him or her feel important."

"Name the top six reasons that people choose a bank."

Your students may not know the answers you are seeking, but their everyday experiences will allow them to give educated guesses. If the answers shown are different from the responses of your trainees, it can inspire a "Wow, that's different than I thought it would be!" reaction that leads them to become curious about the topic.

These types of questions beg to be put into a *Family Feud* game because they fit neatly into the multiple correct answer format. However, they could also be in a game such as *Jeopardy!* or *Who Wants to Be a Millionaire?* as short-answer questions (in this case, limit the number of answers that are required in proportion to the amount of time a player is given to discuss or answer a question).

Other styles of questions that can stimulate thought:

"What is the number one complaint consumers have when cashing checks?"

"Name two of the top five reasons that consumers switch banks."

Thought-provoking questions like these allow trainees to put themselves in the customer's shoes and give plenty of opportunity for a trainer to elaborate on information or segue right into a training session.

To Show Why a Training Topic Is Important and Relevant

Questions in a game show can show that your training is going to be important to your trainees. Let's stick with the banking customer service example. You could ask:

What percentage of consumers who have unhappy experiences at our bank mention it to other people?

a. 20%

b. 45%

c. 60%

According to our marketing department, how much does it cost to get a new customer into our bank?

a. $25

b. $50

c. $150

In each case, you could elaborate on these questions to make them personally relevant—for example, "If 60 percent of our customers tell a friend about a negative experience, how important is it for you to give good customer service?" The trainees can see directly how the upcoming training will be a useful tool for them.

To Make Students Aware of Their Learning Gaps

When you are using questions in a preview, students will make a mental note of how much information they don't already know. This focuses their attention on the training session so they can fill in their own knowledge gaps.

A preview scenario, however, is a bit tricky. You're better off using open-ended questions instead of multiple choice. In multiple-choice questions, if the answer chosen is incorrect, it can imprint on the learners' minds simply by being the first answer read or given.

Something you should take into consideration is incorporating questions and topics that you're fairly certain the trainees have been exposed to. If too many of your questions generate a blank stare, the trainees will feel that they don't know anything at all. This negative reaction isn't necessarily conducive to greater learning. This doesn't mean that you have to "dumb-down" the questions, rather draw them from practical experiences that trainees may have had that support the training topic, and keep the questions fairly general and generic.

These questions should be focused on the information that you're teaching after the game. Using a new example of retail loss prevention training, let's look at how a question like this might be worded: "Greeting customers and asking to assist them can prevent theft. How?" The question is particularly effective if the answer is one that the players don't know because they can brainstorm answers and justify (in their own minds) why good customer service is essential.

In these types of preview scenarios, unless you're measuring results before and after the training session, it is not too important if trainees get the answers right or wrong. You may want to wipe the scores clean after the preview if you are going to continue playing a game in the training session.

Questions to Review a Topic

Since the purpose of a review game is to repeat and recap material, now is not the time to ask trivial questions. At this point, if you throw a lot of information at your students, little of it will stick. The extraneous information won't fit in their conscious brain, even if it is crucial. Don't put any information in there that is not worthy of getting stuck at the expense of more significant information.

A key consideration when reviewing a topic is whether you want to review using recall or recognition. If you're gauging *recall*, you'll want to gauge a trainee's understanding of the material. In this case, use short-answer, essay, or role-play questions. These allow trainees to discuss and apply material in an in-depth way. For example, you may ask: "Enact a scenario where you have to fire an underperforming employee. Use the four rules of hiring and firing that we covered today."

If you're looking at *recognition*, you'll want to gauge a trainee's memory of the material. In this case, use more rapid-fire questions like those in true-false, multiple-choice, fill-in-the-blank, short-answer, and matching questions—for example, "The first rule of hiring and firing is _____." These require trainees to think quickly and answer almost automatically, testing and strengthening their recognition of the material.

Questions to Generate Brainstorming

You can use game shows to generate useful brainstorming and viable action plans. The key is developing questions that will inspire trainees' creativity. These questions are similar to those you would use to generate thought and curiosity in previewing material; you should use open-ended questions that allow trainees to answer freely.

A question designed to generate brainstorming in a leadership training may ask: "What do you think leadership looks like?" A question to aid in developing an action plan might ask: "Once you get back to the office, what steps are you are going to take to increase your employees' confidence in your leadership?"

It's difficult to assign right or wrong answers to questions like this. You may want to put down a suggested correct answer or a few words of encouragement, but the score should be based on the trainees' ability to answer thoroughly. If you are satisfied with the amount of effort they put into answering the question, they receive points. If you want to emphasize the quantity of ideas, you could assign a point value for every viable answer that a team generates or a total point sum only to the team with the most legitimate answers.

Questions to Energize a Training Session

The best questions to use to energize the room are those that can be answered quickly and have a certain element of fun. If you wanted to use true-false questions, this is the place to do it (though you may also use multiple-choice, matching, and multiple-answer questions).

Keep these questions at least tangentially related to the topic at hand so you don't distract the class from what you want them to know. An example of an energizing question in a leadership facilitation course might be: "True or false: Cats exert leadership by rubbing their head against furniture." This question has an element of levity, it's fast-paced, and it opens the gate for discussion later, even though it may not directly relate to your leadership topic.

Questions That Work as Icebreakers

If the purpose of the game is to get trainees to interact with each other in a fun way, ask questions that require them to put their heads together. Open-ended questions work well for this because they take time to think about.

You may also use open-ended questions and direct them at specific people on a team. For example, if you were playing a *Jeopardy!* game and the player asked for "Icebreakers for 200," the question might look something like this: "Name a time in your career when you felt particularly successful." Or it can even be a little more light-hearted: "What was the worst summer job you had as a teenager?"

The trainer can't really assign "right" or "wrong" to answers to these types of questions, but he or she can determine whether the contestant has fully answered the question and can ask the person to elaborate. Questions such as this can also be fun springboards for discussion. For example, if the contestant answers that she felt the most successful after completing a major project, you could ask her what made her feel that successful, what she did to complete that project, or what challenges she experienced along the way to her goals.

For a more spontaneous icebreaker, have contestants write down a trivia fact or two about themselves. These will become questions in a "getting to know you" game. The only rule in this game is that no contestant can answer his or her own question or tip off his or her own team.

Questions for Role Playing and Practice

The key to creating questions for role-play is clarity. The trainees need to understand the setup, the challenge, the roles the contestants are to play, and the results that you're looking for. To be sure the instructions are clear, ask the trainees if they have any questions before allowing them time to answer. You may want to hand out slips of paper with the scenario or keep the question displayed so that trainees can refer to it while brainstorming their answer.

If the training session focused on measures and actions in resolving conflict, a question might look like this:

> This is a scenario between Jane and her boss. Jane feels that Bob, one of her colleagues, has been taking credit for her work and is coming to you, her boss, to file a complaint. Demonstrate the steps you should take to resolve this conflict between Bob and Jane.

Scoring for this question would be based on the correctness of the trainee's actions and also the extent that the player answered the question. You may also choose to award points for creativity or the level of participation.

Table 11.1 summarizes which questions are best suited for your purpose:

Table 11.1. Questions and Appropriate Purposes

	Preview	Review	Energizers	Break the Ice	Practice
Multiple choice	X	X	X	X	
Matching		X	X		X
Multiple answer	X	X	X		
Sequencing		X			X
Open-ended	X	X		X	X
Essay or role play	X	X		X	X
True-false	X	X	X	X	

Using the questions that are best suited to your purpose will ultimately help trainees play the game show successfully and retain the most training content. Another question strategy to enhance and deliver training content is multimedia. We explore the use of multimedia in questions in the next chapter.

Chapter 12

Using Multimedia in Your Questions

In This Chapter, You Will:

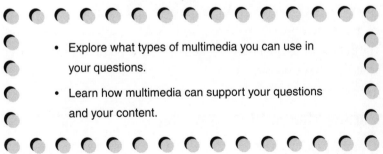

- Explore what types of multimedia you can use in your questions.
- Learn how multimedia can support your questions and your content.

Why Use Multimedia in Your Questions

There are some distinct advantages to using media (audio clips, video clips, and pictures) in your questions and answers:

• *To take liberties with an old saying, "A picture, a video clip, or an audio clip is worth a thousand words."* Some types of information can be communicated more effectively by having contestants listen to an audio clip or view a video or picture (not to mention that these appeal to multiple senses). For example, auto mechanic students could listen to an audio clip of a poorly performing engine and then identify the problem with the engine.

• *Multimedia provides a refreshing break from the all-text question-and-answer format.* The key to keeping a game show fresh is change, and the more elements you have that are engaging, the more enduring your game show will be.

• *Some types of training are best done with multimedia.* For example, if you are trying to teach your trainees to identify varieties of flowers, a verbal description might be adequate, but a more useful example would be a picture or video of that flower.

• *This can be a useful booster for your preexisting training materials.* For example, if you have a training video on communication styles, you can watch a video clip, then pause it and ask questions about it in the game show.

• *Multimedia are useful to help illustrate or reinforce a point.* For example, after you have asked a question and the trainees have correctly or incorrectly answered, you could show a video clip illustrating the procedure they just described or a picture of the product that they have named.

Putting Multimedia into Action

It's relatively simple to put multimedia elements into any game show.

Audio Clips

- Use popular music in a question as an icebreaker. (Be sure to abide by music copyright limitations.)

- Have trainees or new employees recognize the voices of your executives, or have a "guest voice" ask a question.

- Trainees can listen to a "customer" describing his needs and then match the needs with the appropriate product.

- Audio clips are excellent for language instruction. You could have a clip of a native speaker reading a question or passage and have the students answer the question or identify the message.

Video Clips

- Use television clips to illustrate examples of your training. For example, use reality TV show clips to show mistakes in leadership or to present a scenario; then ask your trainees what they would do instead.

- Play a product video after a question about that product to reinforce product knowledge.

- Have "guest stars" reading off or illustrating questions on video. For example, your CEO could hold up an expense report and ask whose signatures should be on the report when clearing an expense greater than $1,000.

- Show a scenario of a customer in a store asking a clerk for help. Then have trainees critique the exchange.

Pictures

- Use a picture of your product, and have trainees identify it or name its features and benefits.

- Show a picture of your executives and have trainees identify their positions, or have them match an executive to his or her title and responsibilities.

- Trainees can identify what a person is doing wrong by seeing a picture of a scenario and pointing out what's incorrect about it. For example, you could have a person lifting a heavy object without bending at the knees or without a weight belt. The trainees should identify the correct position and equipment to lift a heavy object.

No matter what multimedia you use, make sure that your choice is ready to go so you don't have to shuffle around during a game show. This may include transferring cassette-based audio clips to CDs or videotaped clips to DVD so that you can jump to a particular clip if you need to.

Examples of Multimedia in a Game Show

Make sure the multimedia you choose matches the game show you are using:

- A *Jeopardy!* type of game show: Use multimedia for the bonus questions. The television version of *Jeopardy!* has expanded its format to include a "clue crew." These "clue crew" questions feature video clips demonstrating an object, place, person, or other clue that relates to the answer. Another option is to put multimedia questions in their own category or topic. This way participants will anticipate the multimedia element.
- A *Family Feud* type of game show: Students in a call center training class must listen to a short audio clip of a service call. They must then name the top five mistakes that were made, or provide the top four strategies for dealing with the problem. In cases like these, you may need to replay the clip several times to refresh your trainees' memory.

- A *Tic-Tac-Dough* type of game show: Use video clips of "experts" in the *Tic-Tac-Dough* squares to bluff answers to questions (as in *Hollywood Squares*) or to give trainees additional clues or information. If you're using the game show to generate brainstorming, use video or pictures to display an example answer to start the flow of ideas.

- A *Beat the Clock* type of game show: Use video or audio clips to illustrate or describe how a process should be completed. Then have trainees act out the process themselves and give points based on accurate portrayal. You may also have trainees act out their answers and then play a video afterward showing the correct way to act out a process.

- In a *Wheel of Fortune* type of game show: You may use video or audio clips to give clues to solving the final word puzzle. You may also use multimedia in the questions much like you would in a *Jeopardy!* game.

- In a *Concentration* type of game show: Put a large picture or series of pictures behind the matching tiles. You may then have contestants guess the picture, answer a final question about the pictured item, or solve the series of pictures to make a phrase. You may also put a video "behind" the tiles so that when all tiles are removed, a final riddle or question is asked by video.

- In a *Who Wants to Be a Millionaire?* or *College Bowl* type of game show: Have contestants closely watch a video before the game show. Then ask a series of questions based on the content in the video. For example, they could be given a video scenario where they are faced with firing an employee. The questions would detail the proper procedures, policies, and paperwork that this entails.

A bit of multimedia can have a big impact on your game show. Multimedia entertain and engage players on multiple sensory levels. By inserting a few pictures, video, or sound clips, you can greatly enhance your trainees' understanding of your training content.

At this point, you have all the tools you need to select, customize, and add questions to your game show. The chapters in the
next part of the book explore your role as a trainer and a host in
conducting the game show.

Part IV

Conducting a Game Show

The chapters in Part Four give you the keys you need to be a comfortable, collected, calm, and inspired game show host. We're going to look at how to be a successful trainer-host by separating the two roles, first starting with being the host (Chapter Thirteen) and then progressing to the trainer-host (Chapter Fourteen). The rest of the chapters deal with other elements in conducting a game show: setting up for your game show (Chapter Fifteen), using and not using software programs (Chapter Sixteen), and rating your performance (Chapter Seventeen).

Chapter 13

The Ultimate Game Show Host

In This Chapter, You Will:

- Review the basic mechanics of hosting a game show.

- Learn host etiquette.

- Find tips on engaging your audience as the host.

On television, the host has it easy. He or she strolls onto the set looking polished and debonair, reads through the questions a few times to make sure his or her pronunciation is correct, shakes hands with the contestants, and in the course of one day lays down five thirty-minute game show segments. Not bad work if you can get it!

Game show trainer-hosts have a more challenging task. They must control the flow of the game, explain and enforce the rules, assemble and ask the questions, and often judge the correctness of the answers. Most important, they must simultaneously wear the hat of the trainer, using the game show as a tool to impart knowledge and improve content retention. (With all due respect, we'd like to see an Alex Trebek or Regis Philbin type do that!)

Being a good trainer-host is not difficult, but like anything else worth doing, it requires a little preparation and practice. That's something that trainers do on a daily basis anyway, so you've already got a good head start.

The primary responsibility of the host is to facilitate the game show so that it is executed smoothly. We have some recommendations to make you more successful.

Be Thorough When Introducing the Game

Be sure to explain everything before the game show starts. There's nothing worse than being a contestant and not knowing what you're supposed to do, especially if you're being scored. The contestants need to understand the structure of the game, and the logistics: how long they get to answer questions, the number of matches, and especially the rules of play. It's the role of the host to explain all of this before the contestants see the first question. Your introduction should basically explain the components of the game.

The Purpose of the Game

Some trainees will be thrilled to have the opportunity to play a game show in class; it is fun, after all. The more pragmatic ones may wonder why they are "playing games" when they could be back at their desks "being productive." You'll need to address the game show in a way that suits both types of students. You can do this by showing how the game show relates to the objectives of the training session, but in a fun way—for instance:

> "We've covered a lot of ground this morning, so let's change the pace right now. We're going to do this in a way that's both educational and fun by reviewing what we've covered with a game show."

> "Before we dive into this topic, I want to discover what you know and don't know by using a game show."

> "The person who answers this question correctly gets to go first in our game show: 'What is the purpose of playing this game show?' The first person or team to answer, 'To learn about _____ ' goes first."

Game Logistics

Logistics refers to the number of matches or rounds, the match length, the team setup, how the game is going to be played, and the other components. Clearly communicate each of these elements before your trainees get an opportunity to start the game.

It goes without saying: make sure that you clearly understand how the game show is played. You may want to try to explain the game to a friend or coworker before explaining it to your class just to make sure that you're clear and have thought of everything. It's okay to look up the rules and print or copy a cheat sheet for yourself to use during the game.

Material to Be Covered in the Game Show

Only a brief explanation is needed here. Something like, "This game is going to review our new gun policy," will do just fine.

Rules of the Game

It's crucial that your audience understands how the game show is played. Simply saying, "This is just like the TV show," is not enough. Even we don't remember every rule from the game shows (and we play them quite frequently). Be explicit. Depending on the game you play, explain:

- How and when contestants ring in

- How long contestants have to answer

- If they need to answer in a particular way (for example, in the form of a question)

- How scoring will work

- Penalties (for example, for answering incorrectly, cheating, or ringing in early)

- Any bonus opportunities to score extra points

Be sure to emphasize any changes that you've made to the rules. Being clear here will resolve potential problems during the heat of battle and will save you a lot of headaches. If you're not sure that you're coming across, practice explaining the rules to a friend first.

 ### Tips for Introducing Rules

- If necessary, print out the rules and have the audience read along as you explain them. This is particularly good when the rules are complicated. (We've provided sample premade rule cards on the CD in this book. You may need to make changes to these rules accordingly.)

- You may want to go through the rules after the contestants have been introduced to the game—just before the start of game play. This is when you'll have their peak attention because the rules relate to their success.

- Write the rules on a whiteboard beforehand so they'll be visible throughout the game as a reference.

- Remind the audience about the rules as needed throughout the game.

- Play a sample question before officially starting the game show. This way you can demonstrate the rules and how the questions and game will run before there are points at stake.

Work with the Teams and Contestants

You'll need to explain the setup of the teams and introduce the contestants to each other (if they aren't already acquainted). If time permits, chat with contestants before the round or match starts. If the training class is large, ask them to introduce themselves. This is also a time to ask questions about their perspectives on the training—for example, what they'd like to learn or take away from the training session. This will probably take place before you even hint at a game show, but it's a good idea regardless.

Offer Words of Encouragement

Never, ever, ever, ever, *ever* (we mean it—*never*) ridicule a contestant or a team for an incorrect answer or low scores. First, if a contestant is made to feel foolish, chances are he or she will think twice before answering another question, as will the rest of their team. In the worst of cases, the contestant will think twice about speaking up in the training session ever again. Second, learning doesn't happen in a threatening environment. A trainee who is stressed or embarrassed is more concerned with keeping his or her self-esteem intact than with remembering the material.

You are a safe harbor, a nurturing trainer with a sincere desire to help your trainees learn—not someone your trainees should fear. If you watch the pros on television, you'll see that most of them (with the exception of *Weakest Link* type of games) act as if they sincerely want each contestant to do well. When a contestant misses a question, especially if the stakes are high, you hear the host lower his voice and somberly say, "I'm sorry. The correct answer is . . ." Remember to celebrate your trainees' successes and express empathy with their failures.

Periodically Recap the Scores

This is a chance to congratulate the teams that are ahead for their work so far and to remind the losing teams that they are still in the game. Recapping scores will also stoke the fires of competition and keep participants involved.

Be Very Familiar with the Questions and Answers

If you didn't write the questions yourself, make sure you're familiar with pronunciation and phrasing. If you're judging the accuracy of the answers, be sure you know the content well enough to be able to handle an objection.

We always recommend printing out an answer guide. Even the most knowledgeable of trainers can forget what was supposed to be the correct answer once in a while, and it's good to have an easily accessible backup. This is particularly true for *Family Feud* games. Although you may be very familiar with the answers, it's easy to forget the correct order of the answers or where a particular answer is located.

If possible, have content experts serve as judges to handle disputed answers. They can explain rulings, keeping you neutral. Always remember: Whether it is you or someone else, the judges' rulings are *always final*.

Keep the Audience Involved

Get the audience (any trainees or observers who aren't on a team playing the game) to cheer on the contestants so they are always participating. If a team is in last place, you may notice that support has dwindled. Remind the audience that their support is crucial to the teams' success, and lead them in cheering on their team. If there is anyone who is in the room observing, like an executive or colleague, you can assign that person to a team or to be part of both teams' "cheering squad" or you can simply have this person help judge, assist you with handing out prizes, or deal with other matters.

Maintain Control of the Room

In most cases, you want the game show to have high energy with an audience and contestants who are enthusiastic and involved. Depending on your trainees and the nature of the competition, the enthusiasm can border on bedlam. We've heard and seen audience members standing on chairs and hooting when their team scores points—or booing voraciously when the judges count an answer as incorrect. A bit of this is healthy, and in most cases it's okay for the host to just smile and go along with the mood.

However, if the enthusiasm reaches a crescendo that is interfering with the game—the teammates can't hear the question, you can't hear the answers, teams are tottering on poor sportsmanship, trying to cheat, or generally disrupting the game—it is time to rein them in. Here are some tips to bring control back into the room:

- Impose a rule that allows you to deduct points if anyone demonstrates poor sportsmanship or disturbs the play of the game. Explain that enthusiastic support is good, but negative consequences can happen if it goes too far.

- Explain that cheating will not be tolerated. If you laugh it off when the first team cheats just a little, it will only get worse throughout the game. Some trainers choose to allow reasonable amounts of cheating with the view that the information is being absorbed regardless. However, in our experience, cheating is just another source of chaos that you should avoid.

- Diffuse the "winning is everything" attitude. Remind the audience that the purpose of the game show is to teach. Say something like, "Winning is nice, but *everyone* wins when everyone learns." It sounds a little bit like an after-school special and the more jaded trainees will wince when they hear it, but they will get the idea.

- Assign team leaders before starting to play the game show, and ask them to help you maintain control of their team. They can also be helpful to keep spirits high when the team is behind.

- Slow down. Slowing the pace of your game by debriefing and recapping scores, points, and content will give trainees a break from the momentum of the game. In this way, you can regain control without having to act like law enforcement.

 ## Tip: When Good Trainees Go "Bad"

- Dealing with reluctant participants: Sometimes even the best, most well-informed trainees aren't enthusiastic participants in a game show. If you anticipate that a trainee will be reluctant, place him or her on a team of high-energy, more enthusiastic players. Don't put these people on the spot, and allow them to participate within their comfort level. This is usually enough to draw a shy player out of their shell, and a skeptical player won't be able to repel the infectious energy for long.

- Dealing with rowdy players: When a game show gets going, it can get rather boisterous. There are some players who will be very excited. However, there is a point of excess. When a trainee is a bit too enthusias-tic, smile and address the person directly. Gently explain that although you appreciate the support, he needs to exercise some control over his excitement. Remind him of the point of the game: to review, to learn, and to have fun—but these three elements have to be balanced. At the beginning of the game show, you may want to suggest the proper way to act, so that you can refer to this at a later point. If behavior becomes excessive, warn him that he may be asked to leave the game, and if all else fails, ask him to sit down.

  Rowdy players can also be an asset to you. Designating a very enthusiastic player as a team captain can control this person's behavior, as well as improve the energy level of the entire team.

  Above all, when good trainees go "bad" keep your cool. Continue to be encouraging and firm. Don't spend more time concentrating on the "bad" players than those who are willing and appropriately active participants.

Rehearsal

Even the most experienced game show hosts need to rehearse. Rehearsing allows you to:

- Make sure that all equipment is in working order

- Anticipate any problems that might come up so that you can prepare for them

- Practice your hosting skills without the pressure of a large audience

- Familiarize yourself with the flow of the game show and with your own material

Rehearsing before a game show in your training session can save you a lot of headaches down the road. When you are rehearsing, here are some things to consider:

- The best way to rehearse is to practice setting up the game show as if your trainees were in the room. Make note of things like dark areas in a room or seats where trainees won't be able to see what's going on. Figure out where you want everyone (if you're planning on moving trainees around) and, more important, where you *don't* want people. Decide where you would like to be and where game boards and ring-in devices will go.
- Bring a friend in the room with you and go through the game show. Have her act as a naysayer, pointing out what could go wrong. Bring another friend in (either at the same time, or separately) and have him give you positive feedback on your performance and the game flow.
- Walk through the entire game show—not just the first few rounds. This way you won't find yourself getting to the final question and not knowing what to do.

- As you rehearse, include necessary steps like recapping team scores or setting up for different rounds and matches. Include any training material in your run-through that you might add to make sure that your presentation is seamless.

- When walking through the entire game, make sure that nothing will surprise you. Note where you may need extra pens or notecards. If you're using a software program, become familiar with how to run the program.

Playing to Your Strengths

Some people naturally have a flair (like Dan) and some people are more low-key hosts (like Missy). Both approaches can work, and here's how:

> MISSY: Don't play *Jeopardy!* first if you're an inexperienced host. Instead, play a game where you know which question is going to come up next, like *Wheel of Fortune* or *Who Wants to Be a Millionaire?*
>
> DAN: Don't be overconfident, and don't be funny for fun's sake. We had a host everyone loved: he was confident, funny, and engaging. However, he didn't know exactly how to play the game. In the end, his copious use of humor couldn't save the game from a host who didn't know the rules and didn't know the content. The game show was less than impressive.

Being a host can be one of the most enjoyable parts of a game show for a trainer. We've spoken to many trainers who delight in having the lighter and somewhat more jovial interaction of a game show host with their trainees. However, as a trainer, it is always crucial to frame any activity so that the maximum amount of learning can occur. We'll explain ways to maximize learning as a trainer-host in the next chapter.

Chapter 14

Maximizing Learning in the Game Show

In This Chapter, You Will:

- Learn how *you* put the trainer in the trainer-host.
- Find tips on infusing learning throughout your game show.

This chapter focuses on how you can improve audience comprehension and content retention.

Every game show has built-in learning moments when the instructor can elaborate on the topic at hand. You have the trainees' full attention, so take advantage of it by reinforcing critical points. If you work these points into the hosting activities, they may be so seamless that students may not even be aware that they're learning.

Here are the keys to incorporating more learning.

Elaborate After a Question Is Answered

While you may not want to—or it may not be necessary to—elaborate after every question, you can reinforce key points by connecting them with the answer. For example:

> HOST: Name the feature that prevents paper waste in the J-45 printer.
> TRAINEE: The Auto-Stop Trigger Switch.
> HOST: That's correct, and the J-45 is the only midrange printer to offer this feature. It can save the average user $3,000 annually!

Some game show software programs are set up so that you can embed additional content screens for each question. PowerPoint presentations can also accommodate additional information.

Involve the Audience When the Contestants Answer Incorrectly

If none of the contestants answers a question correctly, throw it out to the audience. Simply say, "Raise your hand if you think you know the answer." You can reward the trainee who answers correctly with a small trinket or reward. This keeps the audience engaged and makes them more active participants.

Explain Why an Answer Is Incorrect

If a question was answered incorrectly, gently clarify why the answer was wrong to clear up any misunderstanding. It's extremely important that a trainee knows his or her answer is incorrect, and why it is incorrect—for example:

> HOST: Name the feature that prevents paper waste in the J-45 printer.
> TEAM 1: The Manual Reset Button.
> HOST: I'm sorry, that is incorrect. Team 2, would you like to try?
> TEAM 2: The Auto-Stop Trigger Switch.
> HOST: That is correct. [To team 1:] The Manual Reset Button was a feature on the L-30 lines. On the J-45, this feature is known as the Auto-Stop Trigger Switch.

Ask Contestants and the Audience Follow-Up Questions

Asking the contestants or the audience follow-up questions:

- Tests their knowledge of the topic

- Allows you to go into more depth

- Eliminates credit for blind guessing

- Keeps the audience involved in the game

- Allows you to cover more material in a compressed amount of time

For example:

> HOST: Name the feature that prevents paper waste in the J-45 printer.

CONTESTANT: The Auto-Stop Trigger Switch.

HOST: Raise your hand if you know how much the average user can save annually with this feature.

Introduce a Question (or a Series of Questions) with Training Content

Some questions are inherently more complex and need background information. You can embed learning points before a question is asked—for example:

> HOST: As you know, our new midrange printer, the J-45, has features that will make it the easiest and most economical printer to own. (Pause) Knowing this, name the feature that prevents paper waste in the J-45 printer.

When asking additional questions, keep your original setup scenario on screen (or in a handout) so that contestants have a constant reference. Also, it will help to separate the background information from the question. This eliminates the need for contestants to read a lot of information in a short time period.

Debrief the Class After the Game Show

Ask if the trainees were surprised by what they learned or if they discovered anything new. This is the time to segue into a discussion about their ideas and other thoughts. Have trainees write down five things that they learned from the game show on a flip chart or white board, have them discuss what they learned with their teammates, or have them think of one thing they learned that they can share with the others. Adding discussion helps cement learning by allowing the trainees to form connections between your material and their own experiences and thoughts. Make this an opportunity for trainees to relate to your material more intimately.

Debriefing isn't limited to covering the content of a game show. There are several different things that your game show can tell you about your trainees, the company culture, and the effectiveness of your training session—for instance:

If . . .	Then . . .
Trainees are cheating	Consider if and how the cheating reflects the current company culture.
	Discuss with trainees how they used any means necessary to achieve their goals.
	Ask trainees how the cheating affected the usefulness of the game and how they felt toward their fellow trainees after the game.
Trainees were very excited and enthusiastic	Consider what game show elements in particular got the trainees excited. Did they light up every time they thought they knew an answer? Did they get excited only when they were ahead in the scores? Were they motivated only by the competition in the game? Did they become most excited when they got to perform a physical challenge or speak in front of their fellow trainees?
Trainees worked together as a team	Reflect on how trainees knew more by working as a team than they would have working alone.
	Ask trainees if they can see how they could use their fellow trainees as an information resource once they get back on the job.
	Ask trainees if they learned anything new about how the members of their team functioned and worked together. Did they notice anyone consistently taking over the team or anyone who shirked away from the spotlight?

If . . .	Then . . .
	Discuss whether trainees learned something new about their fellow colleagues personally or if they felt closer to their fellow trainees than when they started.
Trainees are very competitive	Reflect on how trainees can use this competition to achieve their professional goals on the job.
	Discuss when competition was beneficial (it motivated them to win) and when it was not (they got unruly, or the game got out of hand).

Case Study: Using Game Shows to Highlight Training Handouts

We organized a game show for a large textbook publishing company. The audience consisted of independent sales representatives between the ages of forty-five and sixty. One of the trainers told us, "The sales reps don't need to know everything about every product right off the top of their head—and in most cases they aren't motivated to do that. What we really want them to know is how to find the information when they need it."

We built a *Jeopardy!* style game based around the publisher's product catalogue. We lengthened the answer timer so the contestants had time to look through their catalogues after the question had been read. The team to find the answers most quickly rang in and answered the question.

The sales reps were able to get active practice finding answers to their questions in the product catalogues and in most cases were surprised to find out how much information was at their disposal.

Tip: Different Ways to Use Training Handouts and Materials in Your Game Show

- Before the game show, hand out the materials that will be covered in the game, and let the teams review the information ahead of time.

- Allow teams to use their materials as a resource in the game show. This will encourage them to become familiar with using a handbook or manual.

- Use a training handout as a "lifeline" in a game like *Millionaire*.

- Let the audience have access to written materials. Then allow teams to collaborate with teammates in the audience who have access to the materials.

As the trainer-host you have the ultimate power to make the game show successful and effective just by doing things that you would normally do in a training scenario, including introductions, elaboration, and debriefing. Some of the simpler elements of hosting a game show include setting up your physical game show environment, as you'll see in the next chapter.

Chapter 15

Setting Up for the Game Show

In This Chapter, You Will:

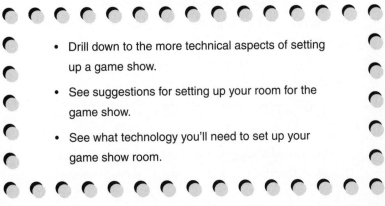

- Drill down to the more technical aspects of setting up a game show.
- See suggestions for setting up your room for the game show.
- See what technology you'll need to set up your game show room.

Room Setup

There are many ways to set up a room for a game show. What will work for you can be determined by the available space in your training room, the number of contestants or teams playing at a time, and the nature of the game. If you can't modify the room at all (perhaps you're in an auditorium and every piece of furniture is nailed to the floor) we'll show you how to work with that as well.

Form Must Follow Function

The room layout must be set up for successful implementation of the game show. This means making sure that aisles are free of clutter and there is a clear path between you and your trainees. Consider seating carefully, but remember that participation is more important than the seating chart. It can be the trainee's view that those who sit up front get to answer the most questions. The truth is that a team sitting in the back of the room (as long as they are able to see) will be able to answer questions just as well if they are being active participants.

- If you're using a computer and projection system to display questions and answers, the contestants and the audience must be able to see the screen easily. Don't give an advantage to a team based on where they're seated.

- If you're controlling a computer and are not using a wireless remote to control the game, you need to have easy access to the computer at all times. And if you're using a low-tech game and don't have a "Vanna White" of sorts to reveal the answers, you need access to the game board.

- If you have more than one contestant per team, teams need to be seated together to make collaboration work. Teams should also be placed far enough from other teams so that they can have private conversations.

- As the game show host, you need to be able to see and interact with the contestants. It is important that you can see everyone in the room, especially their faces.

- When in doubt, rotate. Use less actively playing team members, and switch them out regularly. Move teams around the room each match or round so that no one can claim to be "penalized" by his or her position in the room.

If you want the game show to feel more like a television production, then the room should reflect the audience's perception of what a game show should look like. In some cases, this could mean having contestants on a "stage" or standing behind answer podiums. This is unnecessary to facilitate an effective game show, but it doesn't inhibit game play, and it looks good.

Setup Ideas

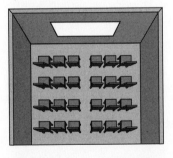

If you're assigning teams based on where they're seated, have them remain at their seats. If they're seated at round tables (referred to as "rounds"), assign one round per team, or move rounds together for larger teams.

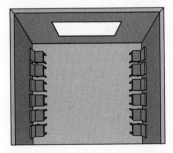

Group chairs together in front or at the sides of the room. This will be your "contestant's row," or the place for the team that is on the spot.

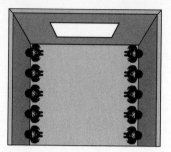

Have contestants stand at the sides of the room if you are rotating them up one at a time. Having them already standing and ready (on deck, so to speak) to go decreases shuffling around during the game.

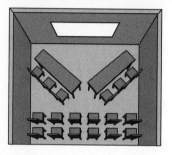

Contestants or teams can be seated at tables in front of the room. Angle tables so contestants can see the screen, or provide them with separate monitors.

In an auditorium? If you're up on stage, incorporate a raised platform so that everyone can see you and the team members who are participating in the game show. You can divide the audience into teams by rows or seating sections. Make sure that everyone in the audience can hear the contestants. You may want to incorporate microphones.

Dressing Up the Room

- Consider putting up banners with the team names on them.

- Put up posters with key points or ideas from the game show. You can even use the question-and-answer format.

Game Show Props

The game show props that we list here are optional. You don't need any fancy props to run a successful game show. There are some, however, that make your life easier or can add a bit of color to your game show:

- Have a leader board where you keep a tally of team scores (either in whiteboard or in PowerPoint format) for a series of games or team scores.

- Use different-colored hats or T-shirts for each team so you can easily distinguish the teams. (This also increases team solidarity for longer sessions.)

- Use balloons or other markers to designate a team's seating area.

- Incorporate host props, like a tuxedo T-shirt or a bouffant wig.

Tip: To Prop or Not to Prop

Props may seem an unnecessary part of a game show. Indeed, the measure of a game show's success doesn't rely at all on having streamers on the side of your game board or a convincing game show host get-up. However, there are ways to make props work for you. For example, in "Dressing Up the Room," we suggested putting posters around the room with key message points. Strategic props like these can reinforce your message and increase visual learning.

Tech Talk

Although we cover multimedia elements in the next chapter, here is a short list of items you should strongly consider having in your training room while running your game show. Of course, if you're using a software program, you probably won't need overheads. And if you're using overheads, a laptop will not be necessary:

- Overheads

- Projectors

- Laptop or desktop computer

- Table or handheld microphone

- CD or cassette players

In the next chapter, you'll get an idea of how to use all of these items to accommodate multimedia, and you'll also have options for creating a more low-tech game show. However, we wanted to present these items here as part of your entire room set up.

The Right Equipment for Your Group

	People	Extra Equipment	Ideal Room Layout
Small group	Two to twelve	A computer if desired	Two or three individual tables with one to four people per table or team.
Medium group	Thirteen to twenty-five	A large monitor or video projector	Four or five clusters (two or more tables joined together) of tables or rounds with three to five people per round or team.

	People	Extra Equipment	Ideal Room Layout
Large group	Twenty-six to fifty	One running microphone (for contestants and host to share), a projector, and a screen	Four to eight clusters (two or more tables joined together) of tables or rounds with six or seven people per round or team.
Extra large group	Fifty-one to one hundred	One running microphone, one lavalier microphone (for the host), and a screen and projector	Eight to ten table clusters or rounds with six to ten people per round or team. For theater seating, have trainees who are in every other row turn around so that they are across the table from the rest of their teammates.
Supersized group	More than one hundred	Consider hiring a professional audiovisual company to set the room up for you or even coordinate the event.	For theater seating, have trainees who are in every other row turn around so that they are across the table from the rest of their teammates.

Almost any setup can accommodate a group, but make sure that the room's size is appropriate. Too small a room will cramp a large audience, and too large a room will intimidate a smaller group and decrease the feeling of community. With a larger group, you may need extra props. A running microphone (a wireless handheld microphone) will save your voice and enable contestants to hear other peoples' answers. A lavalier microphone (a hands-free body microphone that clips to your belt and lapel) is convenient if your group is quite large so you don't have to keep handing the microphone back and forth during the game show.

When setting up the room for a game show, by far the most important thing is for you and your trainees to be comfortable in the room. All participants should be able to clearly hear and see each other and you and be able to interact without the room or setup getting in the way.

You've had a short introduction to some of the technology you might need when setting up your game show. In the next chapter, we'll explore the technology of a game show, including selecting software or making your own game show boards.

Chapter 16

High or Low Tech

In This Chapter, You Will:

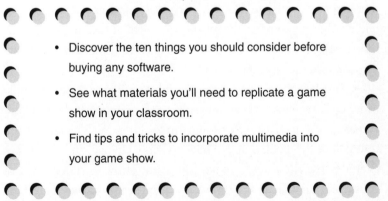

- Discover the ten things you should consider before buying any software.

- See what materials you'll need to replicate a game show in your classroom.

- Find tips and tricks to incorporate multimedia into your game show.

Over the years, there have been a number of software programs designed to make facilitating a game show easy. These game show "shells" allow trainers to input questions and answers and have many other customizable options. These can be useful in providing a rich multimedia game show experience. If you are a trainer on the go, strongly consider using software rather than creating your own game show boards. Software programs can be carried around easily from location to location using only a laptop computer and a small projector.

Software Programs

This book does not endorse one software program over another, but there are particular things that you need to keep in mind when looking at anyone's software:

• *Does the program allow you to create an unlimited number of questions in a library that you can easily import into your game show?* The ability to create an unlimited number of questions is important for trainers who want variety in their classroom, instruct in more than one topic or subject, or work with more than one group of trainees. Questions that you use for one game show won't always work for another game show, but they're not necessarily questions that you want to delete. Having a library where you can interchange questions that you have already made—without deleting and retyping questions—saves you a lot of time and energy and makes creating new and multiple games easy.

• *Is it flexible?* Can you change the number of teams, rounds, timer options, buzzer types, and other components? If the software you are looking at isn't flexible, stop looking. We've emphasized throughout this book that you have to bend, change, and sometimes even destroy the rules to make your game show work for you and your training goals. If the software doesn't let you make important modifications, then it isn't worth buying. Using software shouldn't be a hindrance to your objectives; it should be an aid.

• *Can you embed audio, video, and graphic images into the questions or answers?* If you're going to buy software, make it worth your while. We've emphasized the importance of multimedia in your game shows. Being able to import your own graphics and media into the game show software is a lot easier than having to stop the game play to show a video clip. Why not put it all into one program?

• *Is it easy to operate, allowing you to remain focused on the game play and instruction?* The software program should hold your hand; you shouldn't have to be holding its virtual hands. If the software is so complicated to operate that it detracts from your instruction or the game show itself, then it defeats the purpose of using game show software in the first place.

• *Does it give you flexibility in question types?* Some game show software has options to create only multiple-choice questions, while some are only open-ended. Others allow only one specific answer, and some are more accommodating to a *Family Feud* style of multiple-answer format. One recommendation to keep your game show interesting is variety and change. Having an all-multiple-choice game show is just fine if you're going to play a five-minute game with only fact questions. However, you'll be frustrated with a lack of versatility if you want to play longer or more diverse games. The one thing you'll begin to notice us saying (repeatedly) about software is that if it isn't flexible, then it isn't worth the glitz.

• *Does it enable you to show additional information after each question, enhancing the learning potential of your game?* Your game shows have to be training games, not entertainment games. Game show software should also have features that accommodate learning. A computerized version of *Jeopardy!* just won't be useful unless it allows you to pause and explain key points.

• *Are there different game formats that you can tailor to suit your purpose?* Having software with just one game show format is fine, but variety is the spice of training. Why get one game show when you can get several that are accommodating to several different types of content? Different game shows work best in different situations, and your software should be able to make an easy transition between different types of game shows in your training session.

• *Is the look appropriate? Does it look good?* You might be thinking, *Why is that important in a game show? I thought the point was the learning and not the glitz.* The answer is simple: different types of game show software programs have different types of layouts. Some look very professional and some very elementary. If your target training group is middle-aged corporate professionals, having a primary-colored game with bouncing clowns in the graphics is going to detract from your credibility and the game show's credibility as a training tool. Conversely, if you want to appeal to a group of school-aged children, you may want to look for software in between ultra-sleek and childlike.

• *Does the software company offer tech support?* It's 10:00 A.M., your trainees will arrive in ten minutes, and you want to open with a game show to collect data on what they do or don't know about your topic. All the questions that you input into your game show and saved last night have magically disappeared. Who are you going to call? Discount software programs may seem to be a good deal, but if they don't offer telephone support, then you're up a creek without a paddle. Research the software that you intend to purchase. If it doesn't offer *prompt* support service, pass on it.

• *Is the software reputable?* If a software company can provide hundreds of testimonials from trainers who have actually used the product and have had success, then chances are that the software will also work for you. If you contact the company, is it willing to talk to you (without pushing sales)? Is it willing to provide references and demonstrations? Does it give you a good vibe?

Your top priority when purchasing software is *flexibility*. You need to be able to control and tailor the game show in order for software to be useful for your training needs.

Electronic Buzzer Systems

There are a number of lock-out buzzer systems on the market that hook up directly to your computer and work exclusively with their respective game show software programs. Contestants hit a switch, push a button, or slam down a pad that is connected to your computer. These systems do some of the work for you by letting you know which buzzer was the first to ring in. Electronic buzzer systems are completely impartial and are void of human errors (like not hearing a particular noisemaker or not seeing a contestant raise their hand). If you're using an electronic ring-in system:

- Make sure that all the components are in good working condition prior to the game (batteries charged and in, wires intact, connection secure).

- Tape down wires if necessary to prevent a team from being disconnected in the frenzy of the game show.

- Make sure the slammer, button, or switch for each team's buzzer is easily accessible to all members of the team or the members responsible for ring-in.

- Have the teams test their own system prior to the start of the game to verify that the buzzer is in working order. This can preempt complaints that "my buzzer must not be working."

- Often the team that is a millisecond slower than the others will swear that their buzzer must not be working. When that happens, you may choose to let them test their buzzer again—but this should not occur more than once within a game after the initial buzzer test.

- Remind the teams that the system locks out everyone but the team that rang in first. It may be obvious, but we regularly see the losing team continually hit their buzzer pad looking for a response.

Multimedia and Audiovisual

To use your multimedia, including pictures, videos, and sounds, you may need a variety of different implements:

- **A computer** to run any game show software or to hold multimedia. Computers are ideal to display video clips (often the built-in computer media player can key up a video clip at a certain point), display pictures, and run sounds. The digital format of multimedia on a computer allows editing and quick display.

- **Projectors** to display multimedia, including pictures and videos. Projectors are also useful to have in addition to a computer. If you are running a game show or multimedia off your computer, projectors enlarge the computer images and enable a greater portion of trainees to see the game show and multimedia clearly.

- **Overhead transparencies** to display picture media. In low-tech solutions, overhead transparencies can also do a lot of the legwork in a game show, serving as a game board and scorecard, among other uses.

- **PowerPoint** to key up sounds automatically when you need them in a game show. If you're already running the show through PowerPoint, you can add video and pictures to various PowerPoint slides throughout the game.

- **CD players** to key up sounds, including "guest voices," "right" and "wrong" sounds, and songs or sound bytes. If you can burn a CD so you can easily select different tracks to coincide with a question, that makes things easy.

- **DVD or VCR players** to key up videos, including "guest hosts," video experts, training videos, and other video clips. A DVD player is somewhat more useful for video clips, especially if you're not sure which question the teams are going to pick next. A DVD player can jump to various clips within a DVD, while a VCR requires you to keep make note of the video tracking numbers so you can find your clip when you need to.

Low-Tech Solutions

We're big advocates of using software programs to implement game shows because they save a lot of time and provide automated controls, making your life easier. Putting together your own game shows out of low-tech materials isn't difficult and is a good option for someone who wants to save money or doesn't have a high-tech capacity. In this high-tech world, there is still room for a low-tech experience that will still give your contestants the same amount of information, and an equally engaging interactive experience.

Scoring

This is the biggest challenge in a low-tech game: keeping scores (especially in a *Jeopardy!* game). You may want to have a volunteer trainer or trainee keep scores so you can focus on the game. You need some way to display the scores so contestants are constantly reminded of how they're doing. Scores can be tallied on a whiteboard with a plain marker and an eraser, or you can print out point values (10, 20, 30, and so on) and pin the changing scores on tagboard or corkboard. Or you could hand out a token or ball to the teams for every ten points they earn. At the end of the game, the teams surrender their tokens for a final tally. (This is especially useful if you don't have a co-host to help you keep score.) Calculators are optional, but you may want to consider them for easy scoring.

Timers

Kitchen timers work wonders in a game show—you don't have to constantly watch the clock. Stopwatches and a wristwatch work as well. However, it is easiest to get an extra pair of hands or eyes to help you keep track of time.

Question Keys

Print out your questions and answers on note cards so that you have a quick reference to read questions and judge answers.

Ring-In Buzzers

What if you don't want to or can't use an electronic buzzer system that indicates who rang in first? Don't lose heart; we were determining which contestants should go first long before we had computers:

- Assign an impartial observer the responsibility of keeping an eye or ear open to determine who rang in first. That person should be able to quickly announce the winning team.

- Give each team a distinct auditory or visual ring-in indicator such as:

    Different-sounding bells, whistles, kazoos, clackers, noisemakers, musical instruments, or something else

    Different colored flags to raise

    Different types of sounds, such as vocal noises, animal sounds, or vehicle noises

Whatever system you decide to use, enforce the rule that contestants shouldn't answer until you or the designated judge calls on them. Otherwise a contestant may wrongly assume that she beat out the other players and start to answer.

Be sure that each team has a noisemaker or a way to ring in that is distinctly different from the other teams so that you can discern who rang in first. A quieter method of ring-in, of course, is to have the contestants raise their hands when they want to give an answer.

Low-Tech Game Boards

In many cases there are several ways to build your own game board. We suggest the most common here. Of course, if you would like to construct a more permanent fixture, you can break out the saws and hammers and build your game board with plywood or pegboard. In the Resources section of this book, we list businesses that carry complete or partial game board kits (including *Jeopardy!* game boards and *Wheel of Fortune* spinning wheels). While these may cost some money, it would be worth your time to check out the prebuilt boards in addition to looking at how to build your own.

Jeopardy!	*Materials You'll Need*

- One large piece of heavy cardboard or foam-core board (approximately 5 by 4 feet). You may also use a section of dry-erase board.

- Several sticky notes or recipe cards (approximately 6 by 4 inches). If you have a 3-by-3 grid, you'll want nine cards; if a 4-by-4 grid, sixteen; and so on.

- Roll of tape.

- One dark felt-tip marker.

Using sticky notes or recipe cards, write the point value on the side of the note or recipe card that will be facing the audience. On the opposite side, write the corresponding question. Tape or stick the cards down on a piece of tagboard, and label the category names either above or beside a row of cards. When someone selects a category and point value, take the card down and read the question on the back.

Jeopardy! can also be played with an overhead projector by printing out questions and answers, writing question values and categories on a transparency, and reading the questions out loud while crossing off the boxes that have been selected on the transparency.

Family Feud

Materials You'll Need

- Several large pieces of heavy cardboard or foam-core board (approximately 4 by 4 feet). You will need as many pieces as you have questions (you may want to use a dry erase board for this reason).

- Several strips of paper (approximately 11 by 2 inches). You'll need as many of these as you have answers per question. If you have several questions with five answers each, you still need only five strips.

- Roll of tape or approximately fifteen paper clips.

- One dark felt-tip marker.

Write your answers and their corresponding point value on a large posterboard or sheet of paper. Cover the answers with a numbered strip that corresponds to the sequence of the answer (for example, if "mustard" is the first answer, cover with a "1" strip). Attach these strips using paper clips on the sides of the board. When a team answers a question, remove the strip of paper covering it and add the points that are shown to the bank. You may also use an overhead projector for *Family Feud*, covering up a transparency with strips of paper and removing them at the appropriate times.

Who Wants to Be a Millionaire?

Materials You'll Need

- One large piece of heavy cardboard or foam-core board (approximately 5 by 4 feet) or a section of whiteboard.
- Several colored felt-tipped markers.
- One dark felt-tipped marker.
- One pair of scissors.
- Several sheets of paper (for questions and making arrows as necessary).
- Paper clips.

Create a point "ladder" on a piece of tagboard or cardboard. Paper-clip arrows on the side of the ladder to indicate the team's progress in the ladder. You can also color different rungs to indicate milestones; for example, if a team gets to step 4, they get 100 points, step 6, 300 points, and so on. You can write questions on strips of paper and tape or paper-clip them on to their spots on the ladder, or you may simply read them out loud.

| *Tic-Tac-Dough* | *Materials You'll Need* |

- One large piece of heavy cardboard or foam-core board (approximately 3 by 3 feet) or a section of whiteboard.
- One dark felt-tipped or dry erase marker.
- One roll of tape.
- Cut-out Xs and Os (nine of each), made of sturdy but light material like foam-core.

Create a large grid on a whiteboard or a piece of tagboard. As teams select and answer squares correctly, simply write in the appropriate X or O (if using a whiteboard) or tape on a cut-out X or O. You may also design a more permanent board using particle board with a grid and hooks and foam-core Xs or Os that can be hung on the hooks when appropriate.

If you don't wish to create your own *Tic-Tac-Dough* board, there are several children's games that use a substantially sized *Tic-Tac-Dough* style of board (for example, lawn beanbag toss games), and you may also use overhead transparencies with uniquely shaped X's and O's (one trainer suggests using bottle caps and small sticky notes).

Concentration

Materials You'll Need

- One large piece of heavy cardboard or foam-core board (approximately 5 by 4 feet, depending on how many matching questions you have).

- Several sticky notes or recipe cards (approximately 6 by 4 inches).

- One dark felt-tipped marker.

- One roll of tape.

- A large printout or drawing of a rebus (optional: this can also be done directly on the cardboard or foam-core board).

Although you don't necessarily have to have a rebus at the end of a *Concentration* game, it isn't too difficult to do yourself. There are Internet sites that have rebuses you can copy, or you can make one yourself on a large posterboard. Then tape note cards in a grid over your rebus. Number the cards, and write the questions and matching answers on the backs of the cards. When the team makes a match, untape the cards and hand them to the team.

Beat the Clock   *Materials You'll Need*

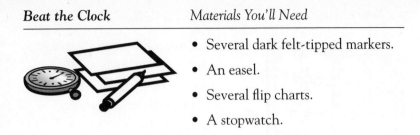

- Several dark felt-tipped markers.
- An easel.
- Several flip charts.
- A stopwatch.

While *Beat the Clock* is one of the easiest games to conduct without software, the construction will vary widely based on which tasks you want to include. If you want to do a quick matching or writing task, you'll need an easel or large pieces of paper for each group. If you are doing more physical challenges, you'll need the appropriate materials. Our suggestion is to do a dry run of the game show to be sure that you have all the necessary materials before conducting the game show.

Wheel of Fortune   *Materials You'll Need*

- Implements of random selection (a dartboard, Ping-Pong balls, or slips of paper).
- One large bowl (optional: to hold your implements of random selection).
- One dark felt-tipped marker.
- One large piece of heavy cardboard or foam-core board (approximately 5 by 4 feet); you may also use a section of dry erase board.
- Several sticky notes or recipe cards.

If you're feeling intrepid enough to build a spinning wheel, you may do so; otherwise take your implements of random selection (a dartboard, Ping-Pong balls, or slips of paper), and number them with point values. Have contestants select their point value by throwing the darts at the dartboard or by drawing from a hat. Draw squares on a piece of tagboard or on the whiteboard that correspond with the number of letters in your word puzzle. If you have more than one word puzzle, it will prove most economical to use a white-board. As the contestants guess letters correctly, you can write them on a sticky note and affix it to the board, or write it in the square itself.

College Bowl

Materials You'll Need

- Two bells or ring-in systems (noisemakers or whistles, for example).
- Several recipe cards (if you wish to write your questions down).

College Bowl is the easiest game to run without software because it does not have a game board. All you need for the game is a set of ring-in devices and your questions (these can be read aloud from your recipe cards). If you wish to print your questions out, you can use transparencies to display questions.

Every Game Needs . . .

Scoreboard

Materials you can use:

- One large piece of heavy cardboard or foam-core board (approximately 5 by 4 feet) and sticky notes with a dark felt-tip marker OR

- A section of dry erase board with dark dry erase markers.

Timers

Materials you can use:

- Kitchen timers, which work well for longer tasks

- Stopwatch or wristwatch

- Alarm clock

Ring-In Buzzers

Options for buzzers include:

- Bells

- Whistles

- Musical instruments

- Sound-effect makers (available at most party shops)

Of course, there are other ways to create game show boards that we haven't listed or even conceived of yet. We are constantly stopped at trade shows and seminars and given new suggestions for materials to build game show boards. Experiment with a mix of software, hardware, self-constructed, and preassembled game boards. With a little trial and error, you can find what type of game board construction will best suit your training scenario.

Every part of the book until this point leads up to playing your game show. The next natural step in this book would be to play your game show. Because of the uniqueness of each training scenario, we can't walk you through playing your game in real time. However, the next chapter takes you through the feedback process after you've played your game.

Chapter 17

Rating Your Performance

In This Chapter, You Will:

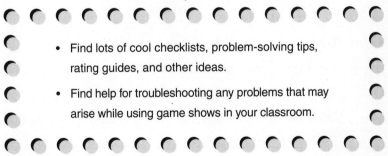

- Find lots of cool checklists, problem-solving tips, rating guides, and other ideas.

- Find help for troubleshooting any problems that may arise while using game shows in your classroom.

Successful Game Show Checklist

In Part One of this book, we emphasized the importance of feedback to your trainees. Feedback for your game show is important too. By critically analyzing what worked and didn't work within the game, the hosting, the contestants, and the room, you get a better picture of how you need to tweak the game show to make it more effective the next time. We know that this book isn't able to give you the full picture of your game show experience. You can get that only through actually playing the game show. Fill out this checklist after your game show is completed.

Learning Experience

_____ Was the game relevant to your material?

_____ Did the questions and answers have extra information or elaboration?

_____ Did the trainees understand why an answer was incorrect?

_____ Did the questions relate to your training content?

Questions

_____ Were questions clear and concise?

_____ Were questions appropriately challenging—not too hard or too easy?

Game Play

_____ Could everyone see the questions, answers, and scores?

_____ Did the game run the planned or appropriate length?

_____ Were the scores relatively even? (There wasn't a complete blowout.)

_____ Did everyone on the team get a chance to contribute?

_____ Did the game end on a higher note than it started?

Judging

____ Did the judges understand their responsibilities?

____ Were all decisions well handled (fair and balanced)?

Hosting

____ Were the rules well explained and understood?

____ Was the audience engaged—even the noncontestants?

____ Was the purpose of the game clear? Did the trainees see the relevance?

____ Were trainees encouraged throughout the game?

____ Did the host have a consistently high energy level?

____ Was the host familiar with the questions and answers?

____ Were disputes or judging issues handled appropriately and expediently?

____ Was the room under control?

____ Were cheating and rowdiness handled appropriately?

____ Was the host composed and prepared?

Hallmarks of a Successful Game Show

- Energy level high throughout

- Scores close until the very end. Usually if there is a lopsided score (one team has 1,500 and the other has –200), it's usually the result of:

  Poor question development

  Poor retention

  Inadequate team selection

  Cheating

Troubleshooting Guide

Symptoms	Diagnosis	Treatment
Scores are very uneven	Teams are unbalanced, cheating may be occurring, teams may have "given up" on participating.	Make sure teams are balanced with more experienced and less experienced trainees playing with each other instead of against each other.
		You may add in point penalties for cheating as a base rule for the game: if a team cheats, they lose a specified number of points.
		To prevent teams from "giving up," make sure that point values increase from round to round, and add in extra credit opportunities and questions where teams are required to wager points.
Low energy levels	Questions are too complex or involved or too difficult.	Simplify your questions to play a quicker version of the game show. A "lightning round" game show will tend to generate more energy than a game show with mostly role-play questions. Mix up your question types within a game to add variety.

Spotty participation	Trainees don't know the material; the entire team (or audience) hasn't been included in game play.	Involve the entire audience by assigning nonplaying members to teams. Noncooperative members can also be assigned specific roles, such as the team captain, to involve them in the game show.
		Participation may also be spotty if trainees don't know the material. Make sure your questions relate to the material that you've covered before.
Unruly group during the game show	The game show overemphasizes competition, has inaccuracies, or contains questions that have no clear right or wrong answers.	Often unruliness during the game show is a result of controversial questions. To cure this, have a friend play through your questions to make sure they are accurate, clear, and concise.
		Installing a judge who has the final word can quell some of the controversy arising from inaccurate questions.
		If your group is unruly, slow the game down in between each question to allow things to settle down before the misplaced enthusiasm reaches a fever pitch.

Symptoms	Diagnosis	Treatment
Excessive cheating	An overemphasis on winning or competition.	Try removing prizes or switch to a more collaborative game approach (with no ring-in).
The game show isn't fun	Several different diagnoses: the questions were too difficult or too easy, the game continued for an excessive amount of time.	Preview your game show before you bring it into the training classroom.
		Have a colleague test the questions, and gauge whether they are too difficult or too easy.
		Keep your game to thirty minutes or less (unless you are adding variety in questions, formats, or something else). Set a timer for your game, and explain that when the timer goes off, the game ends no matter where you are in the game show.
The trainees didn't learn from the game	The questions weren't relevant to the material or were above trainees' skill level.	Make sure the questions you are asking are what the trainees *need* to know versus what is *nice* to know. This way they'll pick up on the important information through the game show.
		A second (and third) set of eyes here is the key. Test your game show on friends who may be at approximately the same level of knowledge as your trainees.

No one answered any questions incorrectly	The difficulty of the questions is too low, or you're a *great* trainer and they learned what they needed to learn.	There's not necessarily anything wrong with trainees' answering all the questions correctly if the game show is fast-paced and short. If the level of energy drops *and* contestants are answering the questions correctly, you need to adjust the difficulty level of questions so that they are more challenging for your trainees. A simple way to do this is to convert multiple-choice questions into open-ended questions.
You hear a trainee say, "This game is stupid"	Don't be fooled; one (or even several) negative comments from one person doesn't reflect on your game show as much as it reflects on the vocalizer.	Treat this trainee as you would an unruly player: take him aside during a break or pause the game for a moment and confront him gently. You can also try making this naysayer a team leader and see if his morale improves with team responsibility. Depending on the severity of the negative comments, you may have to excuse this player from your training session.
The game show moved more slowly than it should have or no one answered anything correctly	Your questions may have been too difficult. Game shows tend to lag when questions are excessively complex or are focused on information that trainees haven't learned yet.	If you realize that this is happening partway into the game, you may need to stop the game and review the material again. Testing your game show out on a friend or colleague can let you know if questions are just too tough.

If your first game show experience doesn't go as smoothly as you had hoped, don't worry. Any new training module or method takes a few run-throughs for most trainers to be comfortable with their presentation, and game shows are no exception. With a little practice and patience, you'll be hosting a game show or a game show that is new to you like a pro.

By this point, you may or may not have had the opportunity to host your first game show. We hope that the game show you create is a pleasant, useful, unique, engaging, and entertaining experience for both you and your trainees.

References

Jensen, E. *The Learning Brain*. San Diego, Calif.: Turning Point Publishing, 1995.

Schwartz, D., Ryan, S., and Wostbrock, F. *The Encyclopedia of TV Game Shows*. New York: Checkmark Books, 1999.

Resources

Research and Books That We Love

Bowman, S. *How to Give It So They Get It*. Glenbrook, Nev.: Author, 1998.

El-Shamy, S. *Training Games*. Sterling, Va.: Stylus Publishing, 2001.

Furjanic, S. W., and Trotman, L. A. *Turning Training into Learning*. New York: AMACOM, 2001.

Jensen, E. *Brain Compatible Strategies*. Del Mar, Calif.: Turning Point Publishing, 1997.

Keeps, E. J., and Stolovitch, H. D. *Telling Ain't Training*. Alexandria, Va.: ASTD Publications, 2003.

Nilson, C. *Games That Drive Change*. New York: McGraw-Hill, 1995.

Prensky, M. *Digital Game-Based Learning*. New York: McGraw-Hill, 2001.

Russell, L. *The Accelerated Learning Fieldbook*. San Francisco: Pfeiffer, 1999.

Schwartz, D., Ryan, S., and Wostbrock, F. *The Encyclopedia of TV Game Shows*. New York: Checkmark Books, 1999.

Sousa, D. A. *Learning Manual for How the Brain Learns*. Thousand Oaks, Calif.: Corwin Press, 1998.

Sprenger, M. *Learning and Memory: The Brain in Action*. Alexandria, Va.: Association for Supervision and Curriculum Development, 1999.

Thiagarajan, S. *Design Your Own Games and Activities*. San Francisco: Pfeiffer, 2003.

Game Show Resources

Although we list a few resources that trainers have found useful, we do not endorse any particular supply house.

Low-Tech Game Show Supplies

Trainer's Warehouse (www.trainerswarehouse.com) offers two sizes of *Jeopardy!* style game boards, as well as several different *Wheel of Fortune* spinning wheels. It also has a Game Show Themes CD. We've found that Trainer's Warehouse is a good place to find trinkets and prizes.

Board Game Central (www.boardgamecentral.com) offers board game editions of popular TV game shows. Although many of the smaller parts would be harder to translate into the training space with a larger class, some pieces may be useful for inspiring your design or with a small training class.

Game Show Software

LearningWare (www.learningware.com) offers a product called Gameshow Pro. Gameshow Pro has six different TV-style games in its software package. The software also integrates with buzzers (also available on the Web site). We've included a demo of the Gameshow Pro software on the CD that accompanies this book.

Trainer's Resources

Workshop

Game shows have been proven to increase content retention and to dramatically improve the experiences of the trainer and trainee in the classroom. A one-day course based on the material in this book, Game Shows and YOUR Training, will show you how to:

- Increase learning and content retention using game shows

- Select the correct game show for your content

- Write more effective questions for your game show

- Host and facilitate a game show from a trainer's perspective

- Stage game shows in small and large groups

Who Should Attend

All corporate and government training professionals interested in improving their training using game shows. This workshop is both appropriate and useful for novice, intermediate, and expert game show users. Sessions are limited to ten seats to ensure that attendees have a one-on-one experience that provides them with real-world training solutions.

You Will Learn

- The brain-based learning theory behind using game shows

- Critical changes you must make to a TV game show to make your game show effective in a training space

- How game shows are powerful learning tools and how to position them as such to a supervisor or trainees

- Training pros and cons for ten popular game show formats and how to select the right show for your training content

- New and diverse ways to apply game shows to your training content

- The impact of writing questions on the success of your game show

- Tips for writing effective and more effective game show questions in formats such as multiple choice, matching, multiple answer, sequencing, short answer and open-ended, essay and role-play, and true-false.

- Different ways to control game show elements to suit your training purpose and flow smoothly in your training session. Including:

  Titling your game show

  Deciding how long your game show should be

  Breaking up the game show into rounds and spreading a game show throughout a training session

  Dividing your trainees into teams, naming teams, and controlling team play

  Setting timers

  Deciding how your trainees will ring in

  Implementing techniques to keep judging impartial and fair

  Scoring strategies to avoid conflict

  Awarding (and not awarding) prizes

  How to balance being a trainer with being a game show host

  Ways to add pizzazz to your game show to give it a more polished look

  Training tricks to constantly infuse and reinforce your content in a game show

  When a game show is most appropriate and effective

  How to avoid the top eight mistakes trainers make with game shows

Participants will get plenty of practical experience playing game shows during the session, and will get to network with trainers from diverse backgrounds.

Here's what previous attendees have had to say about Game Shows and YOUR Training:

"The interaction in the workshop was terrific. I gained LOTS of useful and practical knowledge about being a game show host while training."

"I saw that there were more benefits and game options than just *Jeopardy!* with game shows."

"What I enjoyed most was playing the games while learning the content. It kept me engaged. . . . I know now how important having fun is while learning."

"I have a more global understanding of the use of game shows."

"Great, NEW and fresh ideas, I learned a lot that I can take back and apply to my training!"

"My main takeaway was learning how to phrase game show questions effectively. I never knew that questions make such a big impact on the success of a game show."

Consulting

Dan Yaman and Missy Covington offer their consulting services through LearningWare. Together, they have more than thirty years of combined experience in designing learning-based game shows, making training effective and fun, and helping trainers achieve success in the classroom. We can offer a variety of interpersonal training and mentoring, including:

Game show design. We can design your games using your content, leaving you more time to train. This can include adding custom graphics and tailoring the game to fit your corporate culture.

Staff training. Get up and running faster; we can train you and your staff in game show design and implementation with your new software so you save time and energy.

Technical guidance. We can mentor you through technical implementation, game design, or curriculum integration.

Large Event Design

Live Spark (www.live-spark.com) is a strategic event design firm. It develops game shows and other brain-based learning activities for large events, training rollouts, and customized national training programs.

Index

About the Authors

Dan Yaman has been creating, hosting, and playing training game shows for over twenty years. He has been asked to speak at national conferences, trade shows, and private training sessions about the benefits and techniques involved with playing game shows in the training space. He is cofounder and president of a ten-year-old game show software company, LearningWare (www.learningware.com) based in Minneapolis, Minnesota.

Missy Covington has been writing in all facets for ten years; she holds dual degrees in English literature and psychology from the University of Minnesota. She is an experienced game show creator and has created custom game shows for trade shows, presentations, and national corporate events.

About the Illustrator

Dan Kelly has worked in corporate events and training for over ten years doing Web site design, foil graphics, illustrations, and computer-generated character design.

How to Use the CD-ROM

System Requirements

PC with Microsoft Windows 98SE or later
Mac with Apple OS version 8.6 or later

Using the CD With Windows

To view the items located on the CD, follow these steps:

1. Insert the CD into your computer's CD-ROM drive.

2. A window appears with the following options:

   Contents: Allows you to view the files included on the CD-ROM.

   Software: Allows you to install useful software from the CD-ROM.

   Links: Displays a hyperlinked page of websites.

   Author: Displays a page with information about the author(s).

   Contact Us: Displays a page with information on contacting the publisher or author.

   Help: Displays a page with information on using the CD.

   Exit: Closes the interface window.

If you do not have autorun enabled, or if the autorun window does not appear, follow these steps to access the CD:

1. Click Start -› Run.

2. In the dialog box that appears, type d:‹<\ \ ><\ \ >›start.exe, where d is the letter of your CD-ROM drive. This brings up the autorun window described in the preceding set of steps.

3. Choose the desired option from the menu. (See Step 2 in the preceding list for a description of these options.)

In Case of Trouble

If you experience difficulty using the CD-ROM, please follow these steps:

1. Make sure your hardware and systems configurations conform to the systems requirements noted under "System Require- ments" above.

2. Review the installation procedure for your type of hardware and operating system. It is possible to reinstall the software if necessary.

To speak with someone in Product Technical Support, call 800-762- 2974 or 317-572-3994 Monday through Friday from 8:30 a.m. to 5:00 p.m. EST. You can also contact Product Technical Support and get sup- port information through our website at www.wiley.com/techsupport.

Before calling or writing, please have the following information available:

- Type of computer and operating system.

- Any error messages displayed.

- Complete description of the problem.

It is best if you are sitting at your computer when making the call.

Pfeiffer Publications Guide

This guide is designed to familiarize you with the various types of Pfeiffer publications. The formats section describes the various types of products that we publish; the methodologies section describes the many different ways that content might be provided within a product. We also provide a list of the topic areas in which we publish.

FORMATS

In addition to its extensive book-publishing program, Pfeiffer offers content in an array of formats, from fieldbooks for the practitioner to complete, ready-to-use training packages that support group learning.

FIELDBOOK Designed to provide information and guidance to practitioners in the midst of action. Most fieldbooks are companions to another, sometimes earlier, work, from which its ideas are derived; the fieldbook makes practical what was theoretical in the original text. Fieldbooks can certainly be read from cover to cover. More likely, though, you'll find yourself bouncing around following a particular theme, or dipping in as the mood, and the situation, dictates.

HANDBOOK A contributed volume of work on a single topic, comprising an eclectic mix of ideas, case studies, and best practices sourced by practitioners and experts in the field.

An editor or team of editors usually is appointed to seek out contributors and to evaluate content for relevance to the topic. Think of a handbook not as a ready-to-eat meal, but as a cookbook of ingredients that enables you to create the most fitting experience for the occasion.

RESOURCE Materials designed to support group learning. They come in many forms: a complete, ready-to-use exercise (such as a game); a comprehensive resource on one topic (such as conflict management) containing a variety of methods and approaches; or a collection of like-minded activities (such as icebreakers) on multiple subjects and situations.

TRAINING PACKAGE An entire, ready-to-use learning program that focuses on a particular topic or skill. All packages comprise a guide for the facilitator/trainer and a workbook for the participants. Some packages are supported with additional media—such as video—or learning aids, instruments, or other devices to help participants understand concepts or practice and develop skills.

- Facilitator/trainer's guide Contains an introduction to the program, advice on how to organize and facilitate the learning event, and step-by-step instructor notes. The guide also contains copies of presentation materials—handouts, presentations, and overhead designs, for example—used in the program.

- Participant's workbook Contains exercises and reading materials that support the learning goal and serves as a valuable reference and support guide for participants in the weeks and months that follow the learning event. Typically, each participant will require his or her own workbook.

ELECTRONIC CD-ROMs and web-based products transform static Pfeiffer content into dynamic, interactive experiences. Designed to take advantage of the searchability, automation, and ease-of-use that technology provides, our e-products bring convenience and immediate accessibility to your workspace.

METHODOLOGIES

CASE STUDY A presentation, in narrative form, of an actual event that has occurred inside an organization. Case studies are not prescriptive, nor are they used to prove a point; they are designed to develop critical analysis and decision-making skills. A case study has a specific time frame, specifies a sequence of events, is narrative in structure, and contains a plot structure—an issue (what should be/have been done?). Use case studies when the goal is to enable participants to apply previously learned theories to the circumstances in the case, decide what is pertinent, identify the real issues, decide what should have been done, and develop a plan of action.

ENERGIZER A short activity that develops readiness for the next session or learning event. Energizers are most commonly used after a break or lunch to stimulate or refocus the group. Many involve some form of physical activity, so they are a useful way to counter post-lunch lethargy. Other uses include transitioning from one topic to another, where "mental" distancing is important.

EXPERIENTIAL LEARNING ACTIVITY (ELA) A facilitator-led intervention that moves participants through the learning cycle from experience to application (also known as a Structured Experience). ELAs are carefully thought-out designs in which there is a definite learning purpose and intended outcome. Each step—everything that participants do during the activity—facilitates the accomplishment of the stated goal. Each ELA includes complete instructions for facilitating the intervention and a clear statement of goals, suggested group size and timing, materials required, an explanation of the process, and, where appropriate, possible variations to the activity. (For more detail on Experiential Learning Activities, see the Introduction to the Reference Guide to Handbooks and Annuals, 1999 edition, Pfeiffer, San Francisco.)

GAME A group activity that has the purpose of fostering team sprit and togetherness in addition to the achievement of a pre-stated goal. Usually contrived—undertaking a desert expedition, for example—this type of learning method offers an engaging means for participants to demonstrate and practice business and interpersonal skills. Games are effective for team-building and personal development mainly because the goal is subordinate to the process—the means through which participants reach decisions, collaborate, communicate, and generate trust and understanding. Games often engage teams in "friendly" competition.

ICEBREAKER A (usually) short activity designed to help participants overcome initial anxiety in a training session and/or to acquaint the participants with one another. An icebreaker can be a fun activity or can be tied to specific topics or training goals. While a useful tool in itself, the icebreaker comes into its own in situations where tension or resistance exists within a group.

INSTRUMENT A device used to assess, appraise, evaluate, describe, classify, and summarize various aspects of human behavior. The term used to describe an instrument depends primarily on its format and purpose. These terms include survey, questionnaire, inventory, diagnostic, survey, and poll. Some uses of instruments include providing instrumental feedback to group members, studying here-and-now processes or functioning within a group, manipulating group composition, and evaluating outcomes of training and other interventions.

Instruments are popular in the training and HR field because, in general, more growth can occur if an individual is provided with a method for focusing specifically on his or her own behavior. Instruments also are used to obtain information that will serve as a basis for change and to assist in workforce planning efforts.

Paper-and-pencil tests still dominate the instrument landscape with a typical package comprising a facilitator's guide, which offers advice on administering the instrument and interpreting the collected data, and an initial set of instruments. Additional instruments are available separately. Pfeiffer, though, is investing heavily in e-instruments. Electronic instrumentation provides effortless distribution and, for larger groups particularly, offers advantages over paper-and-pencil tests in the time it takes to analyze data and provide feedback.

LECTURETTE A short talk that provides an explanation of a principle, model, or process that is pertinent to the participants' current learning needs. A lecturette is intended to establish a common language bond between the trainer and the participants by providing a mutual frame of reference. Use a lecturette as an introduction to a group activity or event, as an interjection during an event, or as a handout.

MODEL A graphic depiction of a system or process and the relationship among its elements. Models provide a frame of reference and something more tangible, and more easily remembered, than a verbal explanation. They also give participants something to "go on," enabling them to track their own progress as they experience the dynamics, processes, and relationships being depicted in the model.

ROLE PLAY A technique in which people assume a role in a situation/scenario: a customer service rep in an angry-customer exchange, for example. The way in which the role is approached is then discussed and feedback is offered. The role play is often repeated using a different approach and/or incorporating changes made based on feedback received. In other words, role playing is a spontaneous interaction involving realistic behavior under artificial (and safe) conditions.

SIMULATION A methodology for understanding the interrelationships among components of a system or process. Simulations differ from games in that they test or use a model that depicts or mirrors some aspect of reality in form, if not necessarily in content. Learning occurs by studying the effects of change on one or more factors of the model. Simulations are commonly used to test hypotheses about what happens in a system—often referred to as "what if?" analysis—or to examine best-case/worst-case scenarios.

THEORY A presentation of an idea from a conjectural perspective. Theories are useful because they encourage us to examine behavior and phenomena through a different lens.

TOPICS

The twin goals of providing effective and practical solutions for workforce training and organization development and meeting the educational needs of training and human resource professionals shape Pfeiffer's publishing program. Core topics include the following:

Leadership & Management

Communication & Presentation

Coaching & Mentoring

Training & Development

E-Learning

Teams & Collaboration

OD & Strategic Planning

Human Resources

Consulting

What will you find on pfeiffer.com?

- The best in workplace performance solutions for training and HR professionals

- Downloadable training tools, exercises, and content

- Web-exclusive offers

- Training tips, articles, and news

- Seamless on-line ordering

- Author guidelines, information on becoming a Pfeiffer Affiliate, and much more

Discover more at www.pfeiffer.com

Customer Care

Have a question, comment, or suggestion? Contact us! We value your feedback and we want to hear from you.

For questions about this or other Pfeiffer products, you may contact us by:

E-mail: **customer@wiley.com**

Mail: **Customer Care Wiley/Pfeiffer**
10475 Crosspoint Blvd.
Indianapolis, IN 46256

Phone: **(US) 800-274-4434** (Outside the US: 317-572-3985)

Fax: **(US) 800-569-0443** (Outside the US: 317-572-4002)

To order additional copies of this title or to browse other Pfeiffer products, visit us online at **www.pfeiffer.com**.

For **Technical Support** questions call **(800) 274-4434.**

For authors guidelines, log on to www.pfeiffer.com and click on "Resources for Authors."

If you are . . .

A **college bookstore, a professor, an instructor, or work in higher education** and you'd like to place an order or request an exam copy, please contact jbreview@wiley.com.

A **general retail bookseller** and you'd like to establish an account or speak to a local sales representative, contact Melissa Grecco at 201-748-6267 or mgrecco@wiley.com.

An **exclusively on-line bookseller**, contact Amy Blanchard at 530-756-9456 or ablanchard@wiley.com or Jennifer Johnson at 206-568-3883 or jjohnson@wiley.com, both of our Online Sales department.

A **librarian or library representative**, contact John Chambers in our Library Sales department at 201-748-6291 or jchamber@wiley.com.

A **reseller, training company/consultant, or corporate trainer**, contact Charles Regan in our Special Sales department at 201-748-6553 or cregan@wiley.com.

A **specialty retail distributor** (includes specialty gift stores, museum shops, and corporate bulk sales), contact Kim Hendrickson in our Special Sales department at 201-748-6037 or khendric@wiley.com.

Purchasing for the **Federal government**, contact Ron Cunningham in our Special Sales department at 317-572-3053 or rcunning@wiley.com.

Purchasing for a **State or Local government**, contact Charles Regan in our Special Sales department at 201-748-6553 or cregan@wiley.com.